I have known Ann for several years and found he[r ... *]one to work to the highest standards. This book reflects all the above.*

It is a well organised, informative and detailed guide to writing and publishing a book. The entire process has been broken down and detailed into easy manageable topics. I have no doubt that it will be invaluable to any self-publishing author.

I wish I had come across a book like this when I was writing my first book a few years ago. It would have saved me many headaches and numerous hours of work.

This book is a very well written and greatly needed resource for any author thinking about writing and independently publishing their book.

Congratulations Ann

— Alison Vidotto, CEO, Push! Leadership and Business Training

You guys have been so helpful, so positive, so pro-active, so just generally bloody brilliant, I don't really know where to start. We've ended up with something very beautiful and very polished, and a large part of that is due to your diligence, skill and care. I will be singing your praises to anyone who will listen.

— Georgia Douglas, Editor

An enlightening, easy to read guide to self-publishing; a must have reference for anyone navigating the steps of writing and publishing their own book.

— Dr Helen Dettori

Ann Wilson's "The Entrepreneurs' Guide To Self-Publishing" is exactly what I needed but struggled to find when writing my first book, "The Face Within: How To Change Your Unconscious Blueprint". For published authors there are many fine distinctions to turn good into great, and for first-timers a clear step by step approach to self-publishing from pre-writing planning to promoting that can save you months of frustration and loads of dollars. The book pitch section is exactly what I need right now to pull all my swirling next books into line so they can actually be written and published. Highly recommend it – 5 stars!

— Sue Lester, mindset coach & speaker, www.growingcontent.com.au

Ann Wilson has owned and operated small businesses both in Australia and the UK for over 25 years. For the past decade, Ann has worked in the publishing industry and *The Entrepreneurs' Guide to Self-Publishing* is her first book. This book has been written as a guide to writing, publishing and leveraging a non-fiction book. Ann hopes it offers you inspiration to start writing and complete your dream of becoming a published author.

The Entrepreneurs' Guide to Self-Publishing

How to write, publish and leverage your business book

Ann Wilson

Published 2017 by Independent Ink
PO Box 1638, Carindale
Queensland 4152 Australia

Cover design by Sandy Cull, gogoginko designs
Edited by Michele Perry
Typeset in 11/15 pt Fairfield by Post Pre-press Group, Brisbane

Cataloguing-in-Publication data is available from the
National Library of Australia

ISBN 978 0 9954 1940 7 (pbk)
ISBN 978 0 9954 1943 8 (epub)
ISBN 978 0 9954 1944 5 (mobi)

{ *Contents*

About the Author

Who is Ann Wilson and why should you invest your time in reading this book?

My earliest memories are that of my mother reading to me at bedtime. I would choose my favourite books and she would read them over and over until we could both recite them off by heart. During my lifetime, I have been surrounded by stories, both written and oral, and cannot imagine a life without books and stories.

I experienced a childhood made up of moving towns on a regular basis and the one consistency was family and my books. After high school, I spent a few years working and then took off to travel the world. For eight years, I lived and worked in London, in the advertising industry. I travelled, met my husband, had my first child and bought and renovated an apartment.

Arriving back in Brisbane in the mid 90s, I had three more children and worked alongside my husband, Richard, in our renovation business.

In 2008, I began another chapter in my life's story when I started working at Post Pre-press. Under the watchful eye of Lisa Eady,

I learnt the ropes of typesetting and book processing, along with all the ins and outs of the publishing industry.

Life can throw us many challenges and surprises, and 2012 was one of those years for me. At the beginning of the year one of my daughters was struggling with an eating disorder, and together as a family we had to navigate what was a very difficult and confronting journey.

The medical system has no clear guides on mental health and it was often a very confusing and contradictory path to travel. A treatment that is effective for one person may not be effective for the next. Dealing with an eating disorder was a very dark and lonely place, and it challenged every grain of my existence.

It was during this time that I had a long, hard look at myself and how I saw my role in life, and what direction I wanted to head. Having spent the past 20-odd years focusing on raising my family and working alongside Richard, it was time for me to focus on myself.

This may sound contradictory in nature – shouldn't I have been focusing solely on my daughter? But the opposite was true. Taking time for myself, to develop my own skills, showed my children that I not only valued them as people but I valued what I had to offer the world.

With the publishing industry changing, the previous owner of Post Pre-press, Alan, decided that after 35 years in the industry it was time for him to have a quieter life and so he retired.

In May 2012, I took over the business and began the next chapter of my life, heavily involved in all aspects of publishing.

Anyone that works in traditional publishing will tell you it is a changing industry, and I won't lie to you and say that it has been all roses. When I took over the business we were in a state of change. Our major client had taken all their work inhouse and this left a huge deficit in our cash flow. Restructuring the staffing and moving premises, we all took a gamble and gave it a go.

I consider myself very fortunate to be at the coalface of this changing industry, and I am looking forward to the challenges every business owner will face in this time of change in the digital revolution.

{ *Foreword*

There is absolutely no doubt in my mind that a book can be the single most powerful marketing tool for any entrepreneur and I'm proof of that. Twenty years ago I wrote a simple book called '101 Ways to Market Your Business'. This changed everything in my life and I mean everything.

Today I have 12 books, sold in over 60 countries. I present on a range of topics around the world, I work with giant companies including HP, Google, Hertz and many more. I write and commentate for various business organisations including the likes of Inc and CBS, as a business authority.

None of this would have happened without writing that book all those years ago. Of course when I wrote it, publishing was a mystery to me. Self publishing was just starting to happen and most of the books being produced were terrible. I was fortunate enough to be picked up by not one but two publishers and that certainly helped.

Today, I'm a big fan of self publishing. The world has changed so much and self publishing is to me a much more effective and timely path to go down, for many reasons. Of course we need the right advice to effectively self publish a book and we certainly need guidance. This is where Ann Wilson's wonderful book 'The Entrepreneurs Guide to Self-Publishing' comes in.

Ann has taken what can be a complex process and broken it into simple, common sense steps. She provides a solid framework for writing and publishing a book, specifically for entrepreneurs. Of course Ann also gives great advice for what to do once your book is published, a common stumbling block for many authors, called 'Post Publishing Depression', and it can affect any of us if we don't know what to do after we publish our book.

I've had the pleasure of working with Ann during her own publishing journey. I have no doubt that she is totally committed to helping entrepreneurs, business owners and leaders to build strong profiles through publishing their own book. If you follow her advice, you will have the most powerful profile and leveraging tool and you will have it much sooner than you thought possible.

A huge congratulations to Ann Wilson for sharing her knowledge, experience and wisdom so generously in this book.

Andrew Griffiths
International Bestselling Author and Global Speaker

{ *Acknowledgements*

A special thanks to my family – husband, Richard, and my four beautiful children, Brigid, Tash, Laura and James, who have supported me on the roller-coaster ride of writing this book and who helped pick up the pieces, while ignoring the disaster zone that we often called 'home'.

Thanks to the family I came from – my mum, Mary, and my dad, John, for your love and support; sister, Helen, for believing in me and quietly encouraging me to write this book; Moira, for showing us there is always a different path to get to where you want to go; and my brothers, Peter and Anthony.

A very special thanks to my editor, Michele Perry, who believed in me enough before I commenced writing to encourage me to actually start. Her faith in me has been a huge driving force in getting this book written without too much vino.

Thank you to my KPI family. I have learnt so much this year and I know this is just the beginning. Andrew Griffiths, your kind words about my book pitch inspired me to keep going and just write. My accountability group keep me on track and I feel truly blessed to have met you all.

Lastly, but never least, a huge thanks to my team at the office – Lisa and Ron Eady, Julian Mole, Renee Bahr and Michelle Van Dyk. You are an amazing team, talented and fun to work with, thank you for helping this book be what it is today. I couldn't have done it without you.

{ *Introduction*

As a business owner, do you ever ask yourself, 'What can I do to make my business more profitable, share my experience, and stand out from the crowd?' If you have, you are by no means alone.

The world is becoming a smaller place. When did we become such a global economy? Has it become even harder to stand out in a crowded market?

In 2016, everywhere you look, change and innovation is occurring – digitally, economically, politically – and this change is disrupting the way our lives are led on a global scale.

Global economies are improving, bringing an increase in the number of entrepreneurs to the market place. Changes in digital technology have not only affected the publishing industry, but also how we work in general. It wasn't so many years ago that we would not have dreamt about outsourcing our accounting/bookkeeping to India or the Philippines. Now it is common practice.

How can we, as local Australian businesses stay relevant? How can we compete with not only our local competition but also our competitors on a global scale? It is no longer enough to state, 'I am an expert' on your website and blog posts. We can shout it to the world, but that alone is not enough. To stand out and be visible from those around you, you need to have authority.

Writing and publishing a great book is one way to achieve this.

One thing that hasn't changed with all the advancements in technology is the basic human need and love of storytelling. Within our communities, people often feel disconnected to society and their community, and knowing and understanding your story is a great way to build a connection.

Storytelling is as old as humanity. Indigenous Australians have been keeping their culture alive through passing down their stories from one generation to the next since the dawn of time. These are shared via dance, song, rock art and storytelling. Every culture has their own unique way of passing down and sharing knowledge, and in this ever-evolving world these techniques are constantly changing.

Dreamtime stories are the oral textbooks of the Australian Aboriginals' accumulated knowledge, spirituality, and wisdom, from when time began. Prior to colonisation the only visual form of story-telling was through rock painting. The written word was unknown and the role of the storyteller was not just to entertain but to preserve their culture and educate the next generation of children and young adults in the history, traditional values and lore of the people.

In some ways, this was the first form of self-publishing.

In the early stages, self-publishing was not a credible option, and it was generally seen as something only an author undertook if they hadn't been commissioned by a traditional publisher. This is no longer the case, with many traditionally published authors now choosing to self-publish. The benefits of self-publishing can outweigh the benefits gained by working with a traditional publisher who holds the control. Andrew Griffiths is a great example of this.

Having said that, writing and publishing is no easy undertaking.

Apart from the very real and daunting task of finding the time to write, the publishing process can be a confusing journey to navigate.

Publishing has always been a highly competitive market and an increase in the number of authors choosing to self-publish has unfortunately drawn some unscrupulous individuals to the industry, some of whom are willing to take full advantage of unsuspecting, aspiring authors. Having knowledge of the publishing industry ensures authors stay clear of these traps.

I am the founder of Independent Ink and owner of Post Pre-press Group. Post Pre-press has been working with traditional publishers for over 40 years, helping thousands of authors produce their books. We have seen all the challenges and issues that can arise.

Talking to other business owners, it became clear to me that we all share a common problem – we need to do something to 'stand out' from the crowd and increase market share. However, very few take the steps to write a book.

Here's a breakdown of some of the reasons a small business owner fears writing:

- What if I'm not a good writer?
- What if people laugh at me?
- I have nothing to say that hasn't already been said.
- My English teacher is laughing his/her head off. Remember that C.
- It will cost too much time and money.
- I don't know where to start.
- I have no knowledge of the publishing industry.

And here's some of the common mistakes self-publishing authors make:
- They write without a plan and a framework.

- They honestly don't think they have the right mindset or clarity to write a book.
- They do their own editing and proofreading.
- They design their own cover or use a poorly designed one done by a friend.
- They use amateur internal layout.
- They sign up with a 'so-called' publisher who promises the world and delivers nothing but ongoing fees and commissions.
- They print thousands of books.
- After the book is published they fail to market or leverage their book.

So, how can this book help you overcome these common mistakes?

I have identified four steps in the publishing process, which if done correctly, will ensure that you produce a professional book that you will be happy to promote, while proudly calling yourself an author.

THE FOUR STEPS

Step One: How to Plan and Structure Your Writing Journey

Often the biggest stumbling block for any aspiring author is working out their 'Why', and how to start the writing process in a meaningful and constructive way. This section clearly outlines the steps from developing your 'Why', thinking like a pro, and working with a clearly defined framework and structure. Having this groundwork in place will help ensure the writing process is as smooth as possible.

Step Two: How to Turn Your Manuscript into a Published Book

On completion of the first draft, the most common question is, 'Where to from here?' In the past, self-published books have looked just like that – unprofessional and self-published by someone using Microsoft Word. The key to producing a book that is the quality of a traditional publisher is knowing and understanding all the stages involved. In this step, I share tricks of the trade but also explain what things you can do yourself and which areas are worth spending money to hire a professional. This comprehensive step covers everything from editing, design, print, ebook and digital distribution, plus all the boxes you need to tick with regard to ISBN, the National Library, copyright and so forth.

Step Three: Building Your Author Platform

There is no point in writing a book, good or bad, if no one knows about it. Writing and publishing your book and having hundreds of printed books sitting stacked in your garage is not an asset to your business, it is an expense. Most entrepreneurs will already have a website and a social media profile, and in this step I explain how to build on these existing platforms to build momentum and excitement for your book launch, helping you to drive sales and leverage your business.

Step Four: Leveraging Your Book to Build Business

Leveraging your book as a powerful tool for your business is a step that many published authors fail to get right. This stage covers everything from preparing a buzz around your book launch, to using your book to diversify your business through speaking gigs, workshops, guest appearances and developing your author network for the maximum benefit.

The Entrepreneur's Guide to Self-Publishing is a step-by-step guide to help business owners turn their dream of becoming a published author into a reality. By sharing my knowledge and experience of the publishing industry, I can help other entrepreneurs achieve success within their industry, through the power of publishing.

I also share my own writing experiences – what worked and didn't work for me – based on the research undertaken to write this book, warts and all.

WHY I WROTE THIS BOOK

As I have mentioned, I am passionate about storytelling and books, but I also love people. The entrepreneurs of this world have so much to offer, whether you are a mum and dad running the local shop or a large company employing hundreds of people, we all have a unique story to tell.

This book is written for you. My advice is simple to understand and follow.

I have spent a lifetime living with self-doubt, especially about writing. My fear of putting my thoughts and words out into the world has left me paralysed. I know that sounds ridiculous, considering the industry I work in, but it is one thing to understand publishing and another thing to 'write'.

After a lot of inner reflection as to why I was like this, and the realisation that my fears were based on my own perceptions of my ability, nothing else, I decided to tackle fear head on. My strong desire to share both my publishing knowledge and my passion for storytelling won out.

This book has been written from the learnings of my personal journey, my industry experience, my colleagues' expert knowledge and skills, and what has and hasn't worked for us.

Recently I have undertaken the KPI 40-week brand accelerator course and through this I have met some truly aspiring entrepreneurs. Many are published authors and they all have a similar story to tell. Writing and publishing a book changed their life both professionally and personally.

Writing and publishing my book 'Splitsville – How to Separate, Stay Out of Court and Stay Friends' has had a significant and positive impact on my business. The process of writing itself forced me to really consider the client experience of divorce – the legal

*world of divorce is very black and white, while the human experi-
ence of divorce is full of difficult emotion. That process then
enabled me to expand the service offering of my business. The
book is a wonderful lead generator and has really helped me position myself aside from my competitors. I have just now published
my second book as I expand my business offering into a new space.*

– Clarissa Rayward

So stop thinking and start doing!

We all have our own time constraints and demands of family and friends, and my own true hope is that you finish this book feeling excited and inspired to begin the journey to becoming a self-published author.

In the words of Andrew Griffith: 'Your first book truly can change your life.'

I believe the only way to make real change is to face our fears, ignore the 'procrastination monkey' and get on with it.

HOW TO GET THE MOST OUT OF THIS BOOK

I have written this book following my writing journey, but it is by no means a book that must be read cover to cover.

Some readers will already understand some of the steps in the publishing process and can therefore skip these sections. I have written this book as a journey, but I have included key points and checklists at the end of each chapter.

I hope that you will keep *The Entrepreneur's Guide to Self-Publishing* beside you while you write and publish the first of many books, and that it gives you inspiration and guidance to follow your dreams.

Here's to happy writing, successful publishing and a great leveraging tool!

SECTION ONE

{ Writing – How to develop
and structure your book
writing journey }

{ CHAPTER 1
Finding your 'why'

Finding your 'why' is the first step in writing a great book. Without truly knowing your 'why' and your 'who', you run the risk of writing a book for no one. This chapter looks at the reasons why this is such an important step, and it gives ideas on how you can determine who will benefit most from your message.

UNDERSTANDING YOUR 'WHY'

To begin to understand why you want to write a book, you should dig deep into what the end outcome would mean for you. What is it that you want to achieve, both from writing your book and ultimately in life?

In Australia, we find it hard to talk ourselves up, and I admit, like many women, to feeling very conscious of the 'tall poppy syndrome'. 'Who are we to stand out from the crowd?' But to clearly articulate what the ultimate prize is, you need to define your goals.

Some common goals are:

- Thought leadership
- Business leads

- Speaking gigs
- Advancing career
- Self-esteem
- Fulfilling a dream

While these are all great reasons to begin the book writing process, to be truly successful, you need to clarify the needs of your audience. What are the potential readers' needs? In all honesty, your reader doesn't care about your 'why', they only care about what they will learn from reading your book.

Before you write, you need to understand who your audience is and what their problems are. Simply being your best is no longer a guarantee of being successful. Not so long ago it was enough to be the best service provider in your local area; however, now with the global markets and the internet, this is no longer enough. You need to stand out.

The person who understands the client will always win. Understanding at a very deep level what the client's needs are, will set you apart from the rest. It is not always the best idea, product or service that wins the client, but it's the perceived value that you are offering.

This equates to the success of your book. Knowing what your readers want to achieve by reading your book will be the basis of having a successful book that not only sells well but is a powerful leveraging tool.

Understanding your client's needs takes research, and below is an outline of building up a picture of who your client is and what their deep-level needs are. Not only will this help you write a better book but it will help in all aspects of your business.

Defining Your Niche

Defining and narrowing down your 'niche' is paramount to writing a great book. Writing a book for everyone will have you writing a book for nobody. Your target is not your market.

If a builder who works with both the architect and the renovator writes a book with both target markets in mind, it will end up being a book that is written for neither. Therefore, this book would solve neither one of the niches' problems.

If we use this book as an example, I could have written a book about self-publishing for all genres – fiction, nonfiction, cookbooks, memoirs, and the list goes on. While this has been done, it can have the tendency to be a very general book that leaves many questions unanswered or is very long and comprehensive.

Think about your target customer as an individual person – where are they, who are they, how do they think and behave.

WRITE A LIST OF ALL YOUR POTENTIAL CLIENTS AND HOW YOUR BOOK WILL SERVE THEM.

Niche Pain Points

Perhaps, fundamentally, the most important step in finding your 'why' is understanding your readers 'why'. Why are they going to read your book? What problem are you going to solve for them?

When I was undertaking research for my 'why', I initially thought my 'why' was 'how do I publish a book'; however, by undertaking surveys with fellow entrepreneurs I quickly learnt that this was only part of the problem. If I had stuck to my original 'why' this book would consist only of Section Two and it would not be solving my readers' problems – only mine.

By doing this process, it also led me to understand that of the many reasons entrepreneurs write a book it is seldom because they have a burning desire to be an author; some do, but most don't. It is because they have a desire to share their knowledge and experience, help their customers, and have a wonderful tool to leverage and promote their business.

THE CORE NEEDS

There are general core 'needs' that every person wishes to feel in their life, and understanding these can help you find your 'why'.

'The Six Core Needs' According to Anthony Robbins:

1. *Significance – the need to have meaning, a place in the world, special, pride, wanted, a sense of importance and worthy of love.*

2. *Love and connection – the need for communication, unified, approval and attachment. To feel connected with, intimate and loved by, other human beings.*

3. *Certainty – the need for safety, stability, security, comfort, order, predictability, control and consistency.*

4. *Uncertainty or Variety – the need for variety, surprise, challenges, excitement, difference, chaos, adventure, change and novelty.*

5. *Growth – the need for constant emotional, intellectual and spiritual development.*

6. *Contribution – the need to give beyond ourselves, give care, protect and serve others.*

If you take the time to understand your niche and their primary core needs, you can address these in your book. So not only will you write a better book, but you will write one that will solve very real problems.

At the time of writing this book, Independent Ink assists with publishing books and are currently considering ways to provide a broader service and assist in these other areas.

Everyone has these same core needs but the order of each need will differ depending on the person. Taking the time and trouble to understand these core needs is the key to winning business.

Common entrepreneur 'core needs' are:

1. *Bravery:* To go out in business for yourself takes a certain amount of bravery and a desire to follow your passion and be significant in the world.

2. *Desire:* There is the desire to be loved by your customers for what you do. You have the strong desire to feel connected to them either in person or through social media.

3. *Certainty:* It is often the one great thing lacking for most entrepreneurs. Writing a book is one way of bringing some degree of certainty into your life.

4. *Uncertainty* which rules an entrepreneur's life. And most likely in the start-up phase, variety is your everyday as you are a 'jack of all trades'.

5. *Growth* is a constant, or at least it should be. Everyday owning and operating a business is a learning curve, we learn from our mistakes and from others. Writing this book has been a huge emotional and intellectual development for me.

6. *Contribution:* Being able to contribute to others is often very important to the core values of entrepreneurs.

Writing a book that addresses these core needs and the problems of your niche will have your readers not only buying your book but continuing to read past the first chapter or two. And they will probably follow up by visiting your website, contacting you, and referring you to other people.

WHO ARE YOUR TARGET READERS?

Ask yourself: Their age and gender?
Where do they live?
What is there occupation?
Are they married?
Do they have children?
What is the household income?
What are their values?
Where do they get their information – tv, books the radio?
What are their hobbies?

It can be hard to narrow this down, especially if you are a service-based industry. A business coach may work with businesses across all stages of the business life cycle, but that does not mean each is a client that you wish to work with. There is a big difference between having the target market of struggling business owners, or working with established business owners who want to take their business to the next level.

What's important when defining your target niche is looking at the similarities that your target readers share. There is a saying, 'You get what you pitch for'. If you are pitching at struggling business owners who struggle to pay you what you are worth, then that is the client you will get.

It can be helpful after you have a clear picture of your customer/reader to get a picture of them and put it up in your writing area. When you are stuck, and don't know what to write next, look at the picture and imagine they are in the room with you – what would you tell them?

As an entrepreneur, the purpose of being in business is to solve problems, whether that is delivering the perfect shoe to wear with the dress, fixing someone's teeth, to repairing a damaged roof, or typesetting a book – we are all problem solvers. Your book is the same. You are writing it to solve problems and it needs to be written to solve your readers' problems, not what you perceive them to be.

THINGS TO THINK ABOUT WHEN RESEARCHING YOUR READERS' PROBLEMS.

What are their biggest fears?
What frustrates them?
What keeps them up at night?

Write a list of these problems – 50 at the very least, but aim for 100. Doing this will help you get into the mind of your reader.

Spend time writing this list and then try to group each problem into three or four subcategories. Think: time, money, staff, and so on. Within each group, come up with a clear dominant problem and use these three or four problems to base your book on your readers' 'why'.

Once you have defined your 'why' and your readers' 'why', you will be in a much better position to commence writing your book. Without undertaking this step you may end up floundering during the writing process, as you have no clear direction. Having direction and clarity will help ensure that the writing process is as seamless as possible.

TOP
tips

1. Soul search your 'why'.

2. Clearly define your end goal – think big, be brave.

3. Narrow down and define your niche.

4. Define your niche's core needs.

5. Have a clear picture of your customer/reader.

6. Think about what keeps your reader up at night.

{
CHAPTER 2
Write like a pro

No matter what your plans are for the finished book, you need to undertake writing with the right mindset. You need to think like a 'pro'. Think and act like a professional writer.

The importance of the right mindset can be the difference between beginning to write your book and completing it. How many times have you heard someone say, 'One day I will write a book but …'?

Before pen hits the paper, establish a few ground rules or goals and stick to them. It's not going to be easy, but with practice and determination you can reach your goal.

This chapter covers setting up the right time, place and mindset to write. I also show you how to use 'mind maps' to your best advantage, and most importantly how to ensure 'self-care'. Writing can be a lonely existence and somewhat frustrating. Taking time out to look after yourself is a key element in not only writing a great book but getting it finished.

WRITING SPACE

First things first – work out where you are going to write. Everyone is different and they have their own personal choice. Some people can sit in a coffee shop, away from the office, and write. Personally, I am like a small child and I get easily distracted, so this is not the best option for me. Joanna Penn from the Creative Penn does this and listens to rain on her headset.

I come into the office while no one else is here and write at my desk. Some people prefer to remove themselves away from their work space to distinguish the two, especially if they find writing a chore. No matter where you choose to write, ensure that everyone knows this is your writing space.

WHEN YOU WILL WRITE

This is the time to get out your diary and work out when you are going to write. Have a few practices at writing at different times of the day. A lot of people find getting up an hour earlier and writing works for them. I have found getting into the office before everyone arrives, works for me. I cannot write well at night, my brain is fried, but this may not be the case for you.

Working out times with the family when they can help with school drops offs has allowed me to this. It has been a juggle but certainly worth the effort. And I find that if I spend an hour or two before I go to bed working out what I am going to write about in the morning, I don't spend my time talking to the 'procrastination monkey'.

TARGET WORD COUNT

To be successful at completing your book you need to have a target word count. The trend for nonfiction books has changed over the years, and a good length to aim for now is considered between 30,000 and 50,000 words. Ideally your book should be able to be read on a two-hour flight.

We no longer want books that are long and comprehensive. Readers want to read short, easy to digest books that are to the point and solve their problem.

By having a clear goal for your word count you can easily divide this into the time frame allocated. A 30,000-word goal is 1000 words a day for 30 days. Mentally, 1000 words a day seems much more achievable than 30,000. Don't focus on the final word count, only on the daily targets. And the more you practise writing, the faster you will become.

Set up a wall chart with the daily target listed and record your word count each day. You will be surprised how quickly the words add up and how excited you get about steadily climbing towards your target goal.

HOW WILL YOU WRITE

This sounds like a silly point but it is an important one to work out. Some people find sitting at the computer daunting and that their thought processes just don't flow. Handwriting your work initially can be a great way to dump whatever it is that is stored in your brain. Others find dictating to be a much easier process.

HOW TO SPEAK YOUR BOOK

If you are a very slow typist and the thought of handwriting gives you anxiety, speaking and recording your book might be the answer for you.

A lawyer I know finds this to be a very easy tool to use as she dictates case notes most days as part of her work. If you are organised, it only takes approximately five hours to record a 40,000-word book.

Before you begin the process, you will need to complete your 'mind map' (discussed below), outline and book pitch, as these will be used to keep you on track while speaking your book. If you choose this option, you will need to ensure that all of these steps are very detailed with easy-to-follow bullet points to quickly refer to while you are speaking. This will jog your memory if you come to a blank spot.

How to speak your book successfully is covered in greater detail in Chapter 7.

DISCONNECT TO RECONNECT

This is a saying I have heard Andrew Griffiths use in relation to writing, and it struck a chord with me.

It is extremely hard to focus and write a great book if you are constantly distracted by emails, Facebook, Twitter, and other shiny objects. To stay focused on the task at hand you need to disconnect from all electronic devices. This can be difficult if you are typing your book, but there are several great apps currently on the market.

Ommwriter is one tool available. Their tag line is: 'Re-connect with your friends Concentration and Creativity, and discover the bliss of single-tasking'.

MIND MAPPING

This can be the most powerful tool when it comes to planning what you are writing about, chapter structure and outline.

Creating a solid set of mind maps will make the outlining of your book a much easier process. The mind map is a methodology that will take you from a seed of a book idea to the outline of your book.

If you are unsure that you have the knowledge for a book, creating a mind map of everything you tell your clients, or everything you do in your daily functions at work will give you a clear indication of how much knowledge you have stored in your head. Give it a go, you will probably surprise yourself.

Mind mapping involves both sides of the brain – the analytical and the creative – and pushes you to go through the brainstorming process where ideas begin to flow naturally from one idea to another. To begin the process, use the initial mind map as a brain dump of ideas.

How you create your mind map depends on how you like to work. I found doing them in different formats very helpful. There are numerous apps available, which are either free or cost a small fee. I used SimpleMinds but there are a variety of other software tools on the market.

The other ways you can create your mind map are by using construction paper and sticky notes, notebooks, or a white board. There is no right or wrong way to construct a mind map, it is purely a personal choice. Try a couple of options and see which one works best for you.

Start with your main idea in the centre and from here you make connections to everything you can think of. Initially, there doesn't need to be any flow to the ideas, just get everything out of your head. You can use words and phrases, each connecting to the main idea. And before you know it you will realise how much you already know about your book topic.

At this stage your mind map probably looks like a giant mess of unorganised chaos. The next stage of mind mapping is working out what ideas belong in this book. Some ideas might belong in another book, or perhaps they belong in book number two.

OUTLINING

After you have worked on several mind maps and you are happy that you have all your ideas listed, see if you can see any patterns forming. Which topics naturally fit with one another?

Once you know which ideas belong together, start to work out what goes with what and you will begin to see the formation of chapters.

See more about developing your book structure and contents in Chapter 5.

SELF-CARE

As a wife, mother and business owner, I know only too well the overwhelming urge to take care of everyone and everything else before my own needs. Unfortunately, I have learnt the hard way that doing this has often cost me my own health.

There have been many times in the past where I have worked myself to exhaustion, both physically and mentally, and this has left me dealing with prolonged illness. It wasn't until I reached my forties that I understood the power great sleep has on my health, especially my mental health. A good night's sleep is something I place very highly on my list of non-negotiables.

Time has quickly become one of our scarcest commodities and this feeling of scarcity often leads us to placing self-care at the bottom of our priority list. Who has time to go for a walk or do an exercise class?

Like most things in our life, writing requires both physical and mental space. You can have the most organised work environment, but if your mental state of mind is fried, exhausted and completely overwhelmed your writing will suffer and most likely be uninspired.

Writing a book can be hazardous to your health. Hunching over a desk for hours on end is not good for your back, shoulders or neck. Take breaks every hour for five minutes. Don't check emails or social media on your computer – get up, stretch your legs, go for a walk outside and smell the fresh air.

A friend of mine, Elizabeth, got so caught up in writing her book she spent 12 hours one weekend glued to her laptop. She was so engrossed in her writing she forgot to blink. Monday was not a good day for her. She had caused severe eye strain that required numerous drops daily, her vision was blurry for weeks and she suffered from pain for a considerable amount of time.

If you do not take care of yourself during the writing process, and something goes wrong with your health, it is very easy to cease writing your book. If you are serious about reaching your publishing dreams, taking care of yourself is extremely important.

SMILE

When you write, smile. I know it's sometimes easier said than done, especially if you have set yourself a timeframe for completing your first draft. But believe it or not, writing with a smile on your dial will help you write a better story. It puts you into a more positive state of mind.

> 'Sometimes your joy is the source of your smile, but sometimes your smile can be the source of your joy.'
>
> – Thich Nhat Hanh

Not so long ago something put me in a bad mood, and no amount of positive self-talk could lift my mood. Visiting my local coffee shop, as I do on the way to the office, a small child was talking to his mum and lovingly smiling and giggling at her. The mother returned his smile as only a parent can. The magic of this innocent interaction put a smile on my face and made me realise that life really wasn't so bad after all.

Scientists and spiritual teachers alike agree that this simple act can transform you and the world around you. Current research shows us that a smile is contagious and lifts our mood as well as the mood of those around us. And it can even lengthen our lives.

Each time you smile, you throw a little party in your brain. The act of smiling activates neural messaging that benefits both your health and happiness. The feel-good neurotransmitters, dopamine, endorphins and serotonin, are all released when we smile.

This relaxes your body and can lower your heart rate and blood pressure.

The serotonin released by your smile serves as an anti-depressant/mood lifter. Check out 'Psychology Today' at www.psychologytoday.com/blog/isnt-what-i-expected/201207/try-some-smile-therapy for more information on this concept.

During my life, I have been lucky enough to have some wonderful women influence me and how I see the world. My grandmother was one of them. She didn't have material wealth, but had an abundance of family. During the final stages of her life she was in constant pain, as her spine crumbled with the effects of osteoarthritis. She never complained, much to the annoyance of her doctors, and faced each day with a smile. She was always just happy to play a game of cards, especially if a few coins were involved, or sit (lie in the end) and have a chat. She was an amazing woman, and when I think of her it always puts a smile on my face. When I am feeling down or stressed I will often turn my thoughts to her and ask her for guidance, and she has never let me down.

Writing a book takes a great amount of willpower, the right mindset, and using tools to get you started and keep you on track.

TOP
tips

1. Define your writing space.

2. Define when you will write.

3. Define how you will write.

4. Disconnect to reconnect.

5. Use mind mapping tools.

6. Take care of yourself.

7. Smile.

{ **CHAPTER 3**
Common author mistakes

We all make mistakes – it is part of the learning process. No matter what we undertake in life, it is more than likely we will make mistakes along the way. But is a mistake a mistake if you learn something from it?

From the time you are born you have been learning via making mistakes. Look at how a baby learns to walk. They stand up and they fall, picking themselves up again and trying to stand for an extra second. They repeat the process over and over until they can eventually walk. Some babies learn quickly while others take a little longer. However, the outcome is still the same, the baby learns to walk.

Writing a book can be similar to learning how to walk. It requires a lot of practice writing, determination, and the right mindset to just keep on going and doing it.

This chapter takes a quick look at some of the common mistakes authors make, and it is meant to be used as a guide to help you either see what areas you relate to or things that you can avoid.

FEAR

Perhaps the biggest mistake of all is letting fear rule your life, and by doing this you do not take the first steps to becoming an author, you do not write your book, and you fail to share your unique set of experiences and knowledge with the world.

So many of us have a fear of writing. We all make excuses and sometimes it is easier to find reasons to procrastinate. It is amazing how much you can feel like cleaning the house when you have a writing goal set, or how you just have to clean the fridge because you cannot stand it for another day.

The following is a brief list of thoughts that may be running through your mind. And it's this 'voice' that allows fear to take control and win.

1. *Nobody wants to read what I write.*
   The way you experience life is unique to you and that is your gift. One thing most of us are good at, especially women, is under-valuing our skills. How often do you think of your strengths as being something that everyone else has? Don't undersell yourself and what value you have to offer; someone is waiting to hear your message.

2. *I am not a perfect writer.*
   Most people don't start out brilliant at anything, including writers. Ask most authors who have published multiple books what their first work was like. Most will say it was not their best writing. The more you write the better you will become. Most people want to be perfect and will revise and revise, never being completely satis-fied. Focus on finishing your work. 'Just Do It'.

3. *I don't have time to write.*
   It is easy not to find time to write. I know I have been 'too busy to do it' for years. I suggest starting small. If working in the morning

is best for you, set your alarm an hour earlier and write first thing in the morning – this may mean giving up some TV time the night before. Use a note-taking app on your mobile device to jot down notes on the go or keep a notepad and pen beside your bed to record ideas.

4. *I am too old.*

With age comes maturity and a wealth of experience and knowledge. You may be recently retired or semi-retired and have a lot of information you can share with your industry.

ASK YOURSELF – DOES MY INTERNAL VOICE TELL ME ANY OF THESE THINGS? SHOULD YOU LISTEN TO IT? HELL, NO! IT IS TIME TO STAND UP FOR YOURSELF AND STOP LETTING THAT VOICE BULLY YOU.

'It is impossible to live without failing at something, unless you live so cautiously that you might as well not have lived at all, in which case you have failed by default.'

– J K Rowling

The choice we face is either becoming a failure by default by choosing not to write, or putting our writing out there and seeing what happens. It may fail or it may become a bestseller or a valuable leveraging tool. But it can only do this if you take the leap of faith and publish your book.

Many great leaders face the same anxieties that we all have. The only real difference being that they have mastered the tools to work with, not against, these fears.

Acknowledging our fears can be confronting, and the choice not to listen to them a difficult one, but remember that everyone has fears. With hard work, self-belief and some positive affirmations, you too can learn to overcome your fear. Most people find it easier to listen to their inner critic – that voice that tells us we can't; we are no good; what will people say – you know the one.

You cannot control the final outcome and this is what we often fear the most, the unknown. However, what you can control is the process you take on the road to publishing your book. By reading this book you are well on the way to understanding the journey that lies ahead.

> '*Great opportunities are often hidden behind fear and challenges. If we can move past them, we can discover something that can take us a great step forward in achieving our ultimate goals.*'
> – Alison Vidotto

MINDSET FAILURES

There are countless resources available to help teach you skills on publishing and book marketing. Why is it then that only a few authors achieve great success? One of the biggest reasons is you fail to prepare yourself mentally for what it will take to succeed.

As well as dealing with your fears, you need to begin the writing process with the right mindset, and treat writing as a priority. This was covered in greater detail in the previous chapter. But the most common mistake authors make is not getting mentally prepared to write – tell your family and friends, organise your writing space and writing time, set your daily goal.

> '*The winner, after careful preparation, is confident he will win the war before he wages battle. The losers, without preparation, engage the enemy first, hoping they will win the fight.*'
> – Sun Tzu

NOT WRITING A BOOK PITCH

This is a common mistake, especially among self-published authors. Through inexperience, authors do not understand or appreciate the importance of writing a great book pitch. Writing a book pitch will give you clarity, and it helps set you on the path for commencing the writing journey with the right mindset.

Writing a well thought out and outlined book pitch gives you direction when you are writing, not only on the outline of your book but also your 'why'. Once your book pitch is written, you will have a very clear understanding of the audience you are writing to, your target market and why they are reading your book.

Without investing the time and energy into writing a great book pitch, you can end up writing a book that has no clear direction and is written for you, the author, and not for the reader, solving no problem and having little purpose.

The book pitch is covered in greater detail in Chapter 6.

DON'T TEST THE CENTRAL QUESTION

As part of writing your book pitch you will define your reader's central question. Most authors do little to no research concerning this central question, and they end up writing a book that is based on what the author presumes is the reader's central question.

When Andrew Griffith was doing research for his first book, *101 Ways to Market Your Business*, he initially thought that the reader's central question was 'understanding how to market their business'. But research clearly indicated that businesses didn't care about the marketing per se, they wanted to know 'how to get results from their marketing efforts'. It was only a slight difference but it had a profound effect on the end product.

POORLY DESIGNED COVER

The good old saying, 'Don't judge a book by its cover' does not apply to books – readers *do* judge a book by its cover. No matter what your thoughts are, a well-designed cover is crucial to the success of your book.

Your book cover is your sales pitch for your book and needs to demonstrate what your book is about. An unprofessional, poorly designed cover is not a good reflection on you or your business. The only thing that it communicates clearly is an amateur who cares very little about the finished product.

No matter how well you conduct your business or how well your book is written, people will judge it poorly if it has a poorly designed cover. This not only includes an amateur layout but a cover that does not clearly reflect what the book topic is.

There is no point having a copy of a beautiful boat on a calm sea if your book is about exercise and diet. While you may consider the picture to be beautiful, it may show little relevance to your 'why', and readers will not understand the message you are trying to send them.

Cover design is covered in greater detail in Chapter 10.

INCOMPLETE BACK COVER

A common mistake is giving little to no thought to the back cover. The back cover is the second thing a potential reader will look at and it can be the thing that cinches the deal.

Common mistakes include: no author photo, no price or bar code. This gives the book value, even if you are planning to give your book away. Perceived value is paramount in creating a professional valuable book.

INAPPROPRIATE BOOK TITLE

A common author mistake is trying to be too clever with the book title. Choosing a title based on industry jargon or an insider joke will be lost on your readers. Your book title should immediately let the reader know what your book is about and why they should read it. A clever, funny title, while it may be humorous, may not benefit your book.

NOT USING A PROFESSIONAL EDITOR

Not using a professional editor, or using friend, is a common mistake self-publishing authors make. You believe you are good at grammar and can pick up a mistake from a mile away. Some people can, but in my experience, most can't.

The more you look at something the more you read the same thing, and no matter how many times you reread something you will miss it.

An editor will work with you on:

- The flow of the manuscript.
- The clarity of the structure.
- Ensuring that your text isn't full of industry jargon.
- Ensuring that overall paragraph styles, headings, layout and words are consistent.
- Ensuring that the reader will be able to understand what you are writing about.
- They will check for spelling, punctuation and grammar.
- And they will help you with a whole lot more!

There is nothing that screams 'unprofessional' than a book that is full of grammatical errors, style inconsistencies, jargon and typos. Ask yourself, 'Why would a reader take me seriously, if I can't take the reader seriously enough to spend the time and money on producing a professional book?'

In general, readers are not looking for a literary masterpiece to read, they are looking for a well-written, easy to digest book that will solve a certain problem. Producing an unprofessional, unedited book does not instill confidence to trust you and your business.

Editing may seem to be an expensive part of the process, but it can be a far more expensive problem if you skip this important step.

Editing is covered in greater detail in Chapter 9.

AMATEUR INTERNAL LAYOUT

Using the graphic designer who has previously designed your letter-head and logo may seem like the ideal solution, because they know you and you have been happy with their work in the past. However, it can actually be a huge mistake.

You are probably asking yourself what is the big deal, anyone can layout a book, they all look the same, when in fact you couldn't be further from the truth.

Internal layout is an art form in itself, and it is something that you shouldn't even notice when reading a book. Unlike other art forms, how a book is typeset should be easy on the eye, easy to read and follow. It should not be something that is jarringly obvious.

A beautiful typeset book gives a professional feel and quality to your book. Using a hard to read font, small type and poor hyphenation can all contribute to your book being difficult to read and it will not make reading your book a pleasure. Have you ever put a book down never to pick it up again due to the type being too small and difficult to read?

Internal layout is covered in great detail in Chapter 11.

GETTING RIPPED OFF

As with all industries, publishing has its fair share of 'sharks'. The increase in the popularity of self-publishing has brought with it a number of unscrupulous players to the game, who have no interest in the outcome of the author but only in lining their own pockets.

Unfortunately, this is common among all industries – you only have to spend five minutes watching a current affairs show to know this.

You have most likely poured your heart and soul into writing your book. Having someone produce a mediocre product at an inflated price could most likely leave you feeling deflated with the publishing process and have you put your book in a box in the garage never to see the light of day again.

Self-publishing, and what to look out for, is covered in greater detail on page 82.

PRINT THOUSANDS OF BOOKS

It wasn't so many years ago that there was no other option but to print thousands of books, as to print any less was far too expensive.

This is no longer the case, as with the advent of 'print on demand' (POD), it is a very viable option to print any number of copies from one to several hundred.

You may think that you will be selling or giving away thousands within a year, which may be the case, but I would still advise only printing several hundred in the first months, as needed. This gives you the option to fix any typo that you will find. Every book, no matter how many times it has been edited or proofread, will have a typo or two.

We have worked on books that have reached a six and seventh round of editor's and author's corrections, and still a typo will be picked up for the reprint.

FAILURE TO LEVERAGE YOUR BOOK

In many ways, this will be your biggest failure. You have spent hours on writing, rereading and editing your book, countless hours contemplating your cover design and how you want your book to feel, and possibly thousands of dollars producing your book and then nothing happens.

Why do so many authors fail at leveraging their book? In part, I believe it is because they are exhausted by the project and lose momentum when it comes to leveraging their book.

Also, there is a general lack of understanding that this was indeed the hard part of writing. Ask any published author of both nonfiction and fiction and they will tell you that the hard part of writing isn't the writing itself, but it's in the marketing of the book.

Fear can play a big part of not leveraging your book. You may worry about what people think – will they judge me, will I get bad reviews – the list goes on, depending on your own imagination.

Remember, until you do leverage your book, you do not know what will happen. These thoughts and expectations are only in your imagination. At the end of the day, so what if someone gives you a bad review or doesn't like what you have written. Your book isn't written for everyone, but it is written for your target audience and they are your 'why'.

As with writing, leveraging needs planning and should be scheduled into your diary on a daily basis or, at the very least, a weekly basis. Think about who you can send your book to – potential partners, past clients, media outlets, potential clients. This is a great time to mind map who you know, who your friends and clients know, and what links you have to influential people in your industry.

A common mistake is people don't reach out to media in the right way. Don't send out a generic email to the media – personalise your contact. Research your pitch and understand why your contact should do a story about you. And ultimately, doing your homework saves them time.

As part of the leveraging process be sure to present your book in a professional manner. Whether you are posting your book or giving it away personally, sign the inside cover and include a personal note.

When posting books ensure they arrive in perfect condition. Spend time and a little money on beautiful packaging. A book that arrives in the mail presented as a gift is far better received than a book that arrives damaged due to being poorly packaged.

All authors make mistakes, whether they are writing their first book or their fifth. How do you, as an entrepreneur, avoid these mistakes when writing is not your core strength? By following the four steps outlined in this book you will gain a clearer understanding of the publishing process and its journey. Essentially, publishing isn't rocket science, which is what the big traditional publishers wanted us, the readers, to believe for many years.

It is a process that starts with writing, following a plan and structure, the publishing steps, building your author platform and leveraging your book.

TOP *tips*

1. Overcome your fears.

2. Start writing with the right mindset.

3. Don't underestimate the power of writing a book pitch.

4. Don't presume you know what your reader's central question is. Do your research.

5. Have a professional cover designed.

6. Don't forget about the back cover.

7. Don't be too clever with your book title.

8. Don't use your best friend to do your editing, hire a professional.

9. Don't use your graphic designer to do the internal layout.

10. Don't presume all self-publishing services are equal, do your research.

11. Don't print thousands of books at once.

12. Don't think that writing your book was the hard part, leveraging is where the power of your book begins.

{ **CHAPTER 4**
Tools to develop a framework that works

Before you began to even contemplate writing a book, you probably thought you'd just pick up a pen and begin to write. Magically and effortlessly a book structure and outline for your book would appear – it would just flow from your pen. Well, this was my perception anyway.

For most of us this is not the case. Writing a book takes planning and structure, and this only comes about by working through a process to develop a book outline. This chapter covers some of the tools used to outline your book and give you a clear sense of the direction your book will take.

Mind maps and outlines are a bit of a packaged deal. In order to create a good outline you first need to create a good mind map. Doing so will help you begin writing with the end result in mind.

This chapter explains the purpose of mind mapping and how you can use it to its best advantage.

MIND MAPPING

A mind map, as mentioned previously, is basically just a big brain dump. You start with a topic and put it in the centre of the page.

Then you make connections to everything you can think of. No matter how small the connection, make a note of the idea, as this idea may trigger another idea, and so on.

Before you know it you will have a huge mind map with connections to a wealth of ideas. This process helps gain clarity on how much information you already know about your topic and what areas require more research. Connect the words and phrases, each in their own bubble, to that central topic – building out as you go.

Initially your mind map will look like a huge mess and will need drilling down. You will have words, phrases, circles and lines everywhere.

A mind map is writing without writing. It is a tool that unlocks all the information stored in your brain. It allows another way of thinking and is therefore a very useful tool. They challenge you to think deep and make connections where you may not have before.

There is no right or wrong way to construct a mind map. You can use pen and paper, coloured pens to organise different themes, post-it notes or an online tool. How you work will depend on your personal preference.

I used a combination of all three. I started off using a large A3 piece of paper and then used the online app SimpleMinds to create several different mind maps. I created one for the outline of the book, one for my author platform and another for marketing.

For those of you who prefer to keep things a little more organised and structured, the online tools can be very useful. The added benefit is that they can be accessed anywhere.

The mind map is a methodology that will take you from a book idea to a detailed book outline. It involves using both sides of your brain – the analytical and the creative – and pushes you through a brainstorming process where ideas will flow naturally. Remember there is no right or wrong, just go with the flow.

BOOK OUTLINE

Once you have completed your mind map, the outline for your book almost creates itself.

The key to creating a well thought out and structured outline is to make a smooth transition from what can be a jumbled mind map. An outline for your book is not something that is necessarily set in stone. It is used as a guide and starting point. The following is a guide to turning your messy mind map into a usable outline.

HOW TO TRANSFORM YOUR MIND MAP

The trick is to not feel overwhelmed by the process. Step back from it and focus on the clear themes that stand out. Don't focus on the small topics, these will slot into place eventually.

Organise the common themes together – what topics fit naturally together? These will become your sections.

When I worked on my outline I took an A3 piece of paper and post-it notes. I then wrote each topic on a post-it note and then grouped them into sections.

If you look at the contents page of this book you will see how the theme of each chapter slots together within the section it is placed.

Once you have organised your themes into sections you will be able to organise them in such a way that will make sense. Is there an order that your reader should follow; does one step follow another? This is an important phase in a 'How to' book, but not so important if you are listing 'tips'. With a '101 ways' type of book, there might not be sections, only chapters. From the sections, drill this down even further by organising topics into subthemes or chapters.

In essence, your mind map is a tool used to create a comprehensive outline for your book. This outline will become the checklist you use for writing both your book pitch and your book.

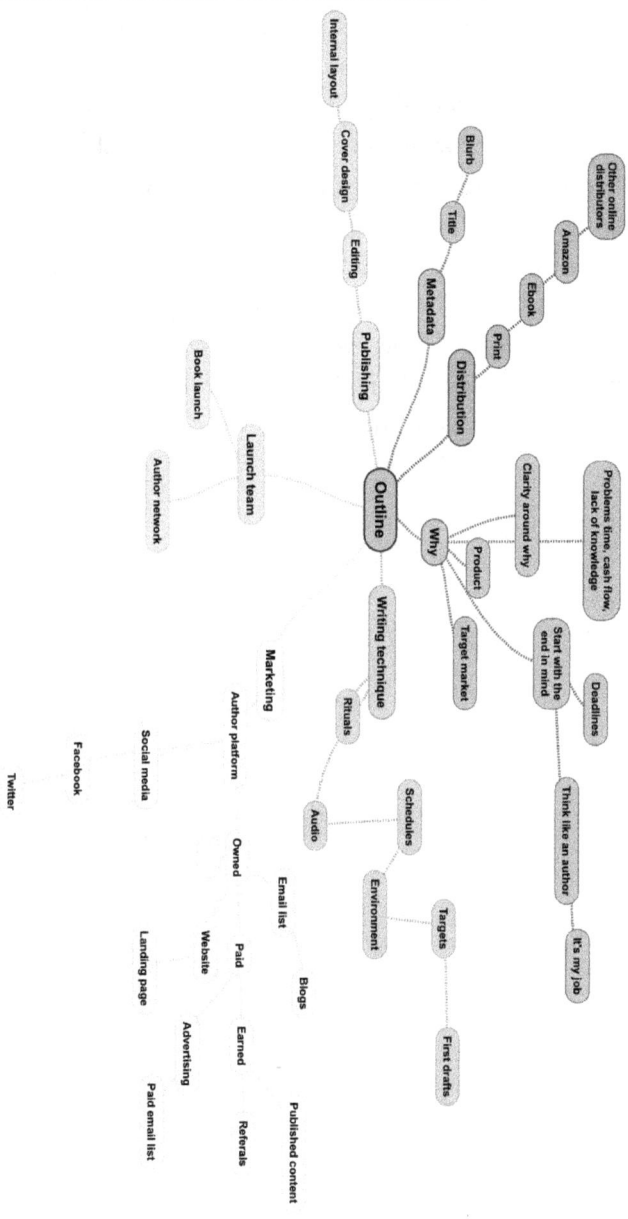

Outline

- Internal layout
- Cover design
  - Editing
    - Publishing
- Blurb
- Title
  - Metadata
- Other online distributors
- Amazon
  - Ebook
    - Print
      - Distribution

- Book launch
- Author network
  - Launch team

- Clarity around why
- Problems time, cash flow, lack of knowledge
  - Why
    - Product
      - Target market
    - Deadlines
    - Start with the end in mind
      - Think like an author
        - It's my job

- Marketing
  - Author platform
    - Social media
      - Facebook
      - Twitter
    - Owned
      - Email list
      - Website
      - Landing page
    - Paid
      - Advertising
      - Paid email list
    - Earned
      - Blogs
      - Referrals
      - Published content

- Writing technique
  - Rituals
    - Audio
    - Schedules
    - Environment
      - Targets
        - First drafts

It is likely that when you do start writing, more ideas will spring to mind. These can be added, but be sure to go back to your original outline to evaluate where they fit into the grand scheme of things. Some of these ideas may not even belong in this book. In all likelihood, when you begin writing, you may have enough ideas to write two books or more.

The beauty of writing a mind map is it can take you from having a seed of a book idea to having a full-blown outline and a clear direction for your writing. It allows you to breakdown a topic or idea in smaller parts and dissect all the information that you have stored in your brain. It is a very powerful tool.

TOP
tips

1. Play around with several different ways to create your mind maps.

2. Don't over think it, just go with the flow.

3. Don't rush the process it can take days or even weeks.

4. Use your mind map to create your book outline.

5. Use your mind map to create sections and chapters that flow.

CHAPTER 5
Develop a book structure

Firstly, to develop a framework for your book, you need to understand what a framework is. The simple definition of framework is the 'basic structure of something: a set of ideas or facts that provide support for something'.

Have you ever read a book that you couldn't really get into? It didn't seem to have any real purpose or flow. The reason for this could be that the book did not follow a clear framework or structure.

A framework for a book is a bit like the framework for a house – without a solid frame the house will be structurally unstable and likely to collapse. This is also the case for writing a book without a clear framework.

A framework not only gives you, as the writer, a guide to what structure your book will follow but will also give each individual chapter structure. No matter what framework you chose to use, own it and work with it throughout the whole book. Don't chop and change throughout the book, it will be confusing to write and to read.

Whichever framework you work with, the most important chapter is your first. And within that, the first page or two have to be amazing. After looking at your front and back cover, possibly reading a quote or two, it is the first couple of pages that will either hook the reader or have them leaving your book on the shelf, quite literally.

To gain an insight into what framework you like, do some research into the books you like to read. Pick them apart and try and gauge which framework they are following and if you can see a pattern within each chapter.

This chapter outlines the various frameworks you can use, and includes examples of books that use each one. By choosing an appropriate framework you will ensure that reading your book will be an easy and enjoyable process to follow.

MODULAR FRAMEWORK

This is a framework that can be used if you have a lot of information to share. Information and ideas can be grouped into similar topics, making it easier for the reader to follow your process.

Section One
    Chapter One
    Chapter Two
Section Two
    Chapter One
    Chapter Two

Example: *Beyond Booked Solid* and *Steal the Show* by Michael Port.

When you are working on your outline and mind map, this framework might become the obvious one to choose. If you find you have a lot of similar topics that can be grouped together under the same section, then this is probably the best framework for you.

SEQUENTIAL STEP-BY-STEP FRAMEWORK

This framework arranges information in a step-by-step sequence. This is the most effective framework for books that describe a process.

This 'sequential framework' helps authors breakdown a process into a series of steps. Each section is a step that readers follow to achieve their goals. It's a bit like holding the reader's hand and walking with them through each step of your process. Each step can then be broken down further into substeps.

This is commonly used for 'How to' books as an easy way for readers to follow the step-by-step solutions on how to solve their problem.

The Entrepreneur's Guide to Self-Publishing follows this framework. I have used four sections and broken each one down into subsections. Each section relates to a different stage in the publishing process.

NUMERICAL FRAMEWORK

This framework organises information or key points in numerical order, often not needing a specific order. Each key point can then be broken down into subpoints. There are many examples of this style of book, some include:

- *7 Habits of Highly Effective People* by Stephen R Covey
- *101 Ways to Market Your Business* by Andrew Griffith
- *22 Leadership Fundamentals* by Alison Vidotto

COMPARE AND CONTRAST

This framework organises information in a way that clearly allows readers to see how two or more things are similar or different to one another. This allows readers to have a clearer understanding of a subject by comparing and contrasting it to a subject to which they already have a good understanding.

An example of the 'compare and contrast' structure is *Good to Great* by Jim Collins. Jim writes about several good companies and several great companies. He then delves into comparing and contrasting the companies, outlining what aspects are similar and what are different. Finally, identifying why these differences are what make some companies good and others great, thereby allowing the reader to gain insights and clarity into how this information could apply to their company or business.

COMBINATION FRAMEWORKS

There are instances when the following frameworks are used in combination with the previous frameworks.

PROBLEM AND SOLUTION FRAMEWORK

This arranges information so readers are clearly able to identify a problem and understand the solution you are offering. This is often used in conjunction with the numerical framework.

For example: if you are getting out of debt.
  Main Problem: Debt
  Main Solution: 10 ways to get out of debt
    Solution One
    Solution Two
    Solution Three etc. to Ten
  Smaller Problem: Smaller problems that led to debt
  Smaller Solution:
    Solution One
    Solution Two

When using this framework, it is important to always present each problem before the solution.

CHRONOLOGICAL FRAMEWORK

This framework is used to organise information around a progression of time. Each main section is representing a certain period of time, and each section can be further broken down into subsections. This is great for helping authors organise information that is best understood by the reader if explained in segments of time.

The 'chronological framework' is often used in childhood development books, history books and pregnancy books. Chronological frameworks can be very effective if combined with the modular and sequential frameworks.

For example: *Up the Duff* by Kaz Cooke. Her book is set out as:
Getting Ready
What's Going On
Diary
Before you Start
Week One
What's Going On
Diary
Making a Start
Week Two

REFERENCE FRAMEWORK

A 'reference framework' is used for organising information that readers will use as a reference book.

Some examples include:

- *Words that Sell* by Richard Byan
- *Modern Australian Usage* by Nicholas Hudson
- *Law and Ethics in Complementary Medicine* by Michael Weir

The key to a great reference book is organisation. Organise your information in as user-friendly a way as possible, allowing the reader easy access to the information they need. At the beginning of the book, clearly outline how your book is organised. Invest in a good indexer to help readers quickly and easily access your information.

There is nothing worse than a reference book with a disorganised framework and a poorly constructed index. If readers cannot quickly find the information they need, they will move onto another book.

THREE ACT STRUCTURE

This is the standard framework for telling stories and jokes.

Act 1 Given Circumstances, time, setting, place
Act 2 The Meat of the story
Act 3 The Resolution and what is coming next

This is not an easy framework to follow for new authors due to its complexity.

For example: *Think Big Manifesto* by Michael Polt.

THE BIG IDEA BOOK

A 'big idea book' takes a single idea and turns it into a short book that explores and analyses the idea through both anecdotes and evidence.

For example: *Tribes: We Need You to Lead Us* by Seth Godin.

These books are generally not complex, simply presenting an idea and making them very accessible and easy for readers to digest.

How you structure your book should become clear from the mind mapping and outlining process but may require some further research. If you are unclear and confused read competitor books or similar topics and deconstruct them to see what works and what you like. In some cases the structure will be glaringly obvious or be a combination. The hard and fast rule for success is pick a structure and stick to it throughout the book.

TOP
tips

1. Research competitor books.

2. Look out for structure when reading and take note of what works.

3. Establish your framework from your book outline.

4. Be organised, don't start writing without a clear plan.

5. Decide on a structure and stick to it.

CHAPTER 6
What makes a great book pitch?

If I am honest, I will admit to being dubious to the importance of writing a book pitch or book proposal, as it is sometimes referred to. Why not just get stuck in and write this book? Why waste my valuable time? But if I learnt nothing else from my past mistakes, I have learnt to listen to those who have walked the path before me, and I heeded the advice of my teacher, the legendary, Andrew Griffiths.

And lo and behold he was right. In writing my book pitch, I gained a tremendous amount of insight and clarity into why I was writing my book, who I was writing it for, and what I was writing about.

Having worked through the previous chapters you should now be clear, or at least clearer, on your 'why', have clarity on who you are writing this book for, and know what type of book you are going to write.

A book pitch is essentially a plan – another format that shows you that you have done your homework and are ready to write. This is standard practice in the traditional publishing world.

This chapter looks at the importance of writing a book pitch and what to include, outlining easy to understand steps that will have your book pitch written in no time.

WHY WRITE A BOOK PITCH?

Why write a book pitch if you are self-publishing? Most self-published authors don't, and this shows in the finished product. You can end up with a book that is lacking clarity and direction.

In a nutshell, as a self-published author you are acting as both author and publisher. By writing a great book pitch, you as the author have confidence in your book ideas, know it has an audience, and have the knowledge that you have the content to write the book.

As the publisher, you have the clarity that the forthcoming manuscript has the potential to not only sell well but be a valuable leveraging tool for you and your business.

I know from my experience, writing the book pitch gave me a very clear direction of what I was writing. Initially, I was only writing about the publishing process; however, through research I gained the clarity around the idea of writing about the processes involved 'before' and 'after' publishing. It helped me gain tremendous insight into my target market and gave me confidence to begin writing.

Getting positive feedback from my peers and Andrew Griffiths gave me enormous confidence to begin this writing process. Secretly, I have harboured thoughts on being able to write for years, but I have never had the self-confidence to show anyone what I have written.

> *'To run a successful business, you need a business plan. To write*
> *a successful nonfiction book, you need a book proposal.'*
> – Barry Silverstein – Business writer, author and reviewer.

Barry Silverstein states on his blog 'Forward Review' that when he reviews nonfiction books, he can easily identify those for which no proposal was written.

In essence, the pitch forces the author to discern whether a dream can be turned to reality or if it is just a pipe dream. Writing one can prevent an author from pursuing an ill-founded concept, and save them hours of wasted time slaving over a hot manuscript.

WHAT SHOULD BE INCLUDED IN A BOOK PITCH?

A pitch tells the publisher/reader why they should read your story. Whereas, a synopsis answers the question of 'What is the story'.

If you can't write a decent 3000-word book pitch and synopsis, you are probably going to struggle with writing a great book. You do not need any fancy programs to start your book pitch, just write it up in a word document and follow these simple steps.

1. Working Title

This is not necessarily the finished title but something to work with. Including a tag line is a great idea. A tag line gives the reader a clear indication of what they are going to benefit from by reading your book.

Having a working title and tag line gives you a title to tell people when you talk to them about the book you are writing. It is also a good way to gauge their reaction as to whether the title is catchy and delivers what you want to deliver. If you find yourself having to explain exactly what the book is about, you may have been too gimmicky, used industry jargon or tried to be too clever.

These are the working titles I included in my pitch:

1. The Entrepreneurs' Guide to Self-Publishing – How to Write, Publish and Leverage Your Business Book

2. Leverage Your Business through the Power of Publishing – How to Stand Out in a Crowded Market

3. How to Become an Influential Thought Leader by Publishing Your Business Book

4. Why I Wrote a Business Book and Why You Should Too

5. There is a Book in You: Become an Industry Thought Leader by Publishing Your First Book

2. Define Your Target Market

This seems self-explanatory but it amazed me how much clarity I gained from doing this exercise. In my business of self-publishing it is very easy to think of my target market as anyone who has or is considering writing and self-publishing. But I had to get my head around the thought 'my market is not my target'.

Understanding this gave me the clarity to write this book for the niche: established business owners who have the desire to take their business to the next level and who are researching effective ways that will ensure they become an influential thought leader in their chosen industry.

Clearly define your target market in three to four paragraphs. This will ensure that you truly understand who you are writing for. I also had a picture printed out and up on my office wall to remind me who my target market was.

3. What is the Central Question that Your Book is Going to Answer?

This is perhaps one of the most important parts of your book pitch. If you cannot clearly identify what your reader's central question is, then you may end up writing a book for you, the author, not the reader. There is little point in writing a book about what you think is needed, you need to ask yourself what are the questions the readers are asking? What things are keeping them up at night?

This was my central question:

What can I do to make my business more profitable, share my experience and stand out from the crowd?

4. How Have You Tested Your Central Question with Your Target Market?

This is the stage where you approach your target market and ask questions around your central question. This is an important stage as you may be planning to write a book that doesn't meet the needs of your reader.

There is no point writing a book solely on 'dieting' if your target market wants to know about how to keep the weight off after they have dieted. There are numerous ways to conduct this research, and this will depend on who your target market is.

You can try:

- Surveys
- Interviews
- Networking Groups
- Client Base

5. About This Book

In four to five paragraphs, clearly define what this book will be all about.

6. What Makes This Book Unique?

Read other books on your book topic – as many as possible. It's not cheating, it is valuable research. If your direct competitor has written a book, buy it and read it. Also, look at blog posts, the media and any other written material. This will give you a clear indication if there is something missing from the market, and it will give you a clear understanding on how you can make your book different.

And remember, you are unique and you are writing this book from your own unique, individual experiences.

7. What Problems Will Your Book Be Solving?

This is a very important step in understanding the reader and why they would want to read your book. Being clear about the reader's problems and how your book can help them will ensure you write a great meaningful book – for the reader.

8. What Is the Ultimate Benefit to the Reader?

As a writer you need to get across to the reader the promise of what reading this book will deliver on. Having a clearly defined ultimate benefit will help in achieving this. At the end of the day, is the reader feeling excited and ready to move forward after finishing your book, or are they feeling overwhelmed and confused?

9. Competitor Books

Like Step 6, do your research. Buy competitors' books and read them. Don't be afraid, be aware and make your book different – you are unique. In my case, I am Australian, this book is current, and the list goes on.

Do not skimp on this research. Having a full understanding of the competition and their strengths and weaknesses will help you write a better book. Very few nonfiction books have no competition, and if your topic is so unusual, you may need to question if there is a market for your book. If there is little competition then your target market research is even more paramount to conduct extensively. Don't limit yourself to books, Google your topic and the problem it solves.

10. About the Author

This is the time to sell yourself, pitch yourself, and ensure your reader knows why they can trust you.

As an Australian, this can be hard to do, as we have all heard of the 'tall poppy syndrome'. I have known some wonderful, highly intelligent, well-educated people who struggle to 'sell themselves'.

I know a lawyer who has been a partner and an owner of a law practice for over seven years but struggled with clearly articulating this. She was concerned with being perceived as being pompous. She works incredibly hard, runs a great practice and still feels the need to play her achievements down.

Don't fall into this trap, now is the time to sell yourself, both to the reader and to yourself.

11. Draft Contents Page

This is where you clearly outline what it is you are going to cover in your book. I found that mind mapping this stage helped me gain clarity. For other steps, I used an app. I also found post-it notes and a large piece of paper worked best for drafting my contents page, as I could move things around and sit back and look at it for a while, until I was happy with the order. This is only a draft and you can add and delete when the writing process begins.

Things to consider when working on your contents page:

- Follow an order.
- Write creative chapter titles.
- Break your book into segments or steps.
- Include an introduction, about the author, acknowledgements and an index if you are using one.

If you are stuck on how to begin, look at your competitors' books for ideas on how they structured their book. But remember, you are not trying to reinvent the wheel. Once your contents page is written it is easy to write your book from this draft.

12. Back Cover Blurb

While not completely necessary to include at this stage, as it will change after you have written the book, it is a fun process to do and makes the writing process seem even more real. The back cover blurb can be harder to write than the book. It is a different style of writing that needs to tell the reader quickly and clearly what your book is going to deliver to them. Start with a couple of questions – identify the problem and the solution. You can also include a quote and an inspirational message.

13. Synopsis

The synopsis, unlike the back cover blurb, answers the question of what story your book is telling. This is the section you can use to send to media outlets if you are asked what your book is about.

Write the synopsis in the third person. Start with an introduction to what you are writing about. Introduce the opportunity, the problem and your solution. Go deeper into the problems and provide the solution. End with a strong call to action. Your synopsis should be around 1000 words, and if you struggle to write a 1000-word synopsis you may not be ready to write a great book. Also include your name and contact details at the end.

14. How Are You Going to Promote This Book?

There is no point writing this book unless you have a clear understanding as to how you are going to promote it. Ideally the promotion starts now, while you are writing this book. Start telling people as soon as you start the book pitch that you are writing a book. It is amazing how much more compelled you are to follow through with writing if you actually tell people.

One quick and easy way to begin this promotion is to include the working title and publish date on your email signature. Write blog posts about your book, and either use content that is being included or blog about the writing process.

Do a mind map on all the ways you can promote your book. Think about your networks. Which associations do you belong to, social media groups, email lists, do you write for any media networks etc.?

The clearer you are on these sources the easier it is to begin promoting your book, and it is never too early to start. Writing and publishing the best book you can, the better the leveraging tool it will be.

Now, I know what you are thinking – 'This sounds like an awful lot of work'. And yes, it is, but believe me it's worth it.

Your book pitch is essentially a business plan for your book. Would you start a new business without a business plan or clear direction where you are headed? This isn't something you can put together in an afternoon; it can take weeks! However, the benefits to writing a solid pitch are enormous, not only for creating a great book but because different pitch aspects can be used in a variety of ways during the writing and promotion of your book.

Book pitches are used to sell nonfiction books to publishers. Marc, a member of my business accountability group, sent his book pitch to several publishers all of which showed an interest and made comment on how detailed and extensive his pitch was. He has now signed a deal with a publisher for a 100,000-word book and is looking at follow-up books for next year.

Imagine, for a moment, you are at a party talking to a stranger about the book you are writing and they ask, 'What is it about?' What is your response? Do you fumble for an answer or have you got absolute clarity? As an aspiring author, you will be asked this question many times. Often people will just be showing interest but sometimes people who ask may be crucial to your book's success and the success you can achieve by leveraging it. Having a book pitch written means you can easily send this to anyone.

As you can see there are many wonderful benefits for writing a compelling book pitch and the greatest one by far is the clarity you will gain by undertaking this step.

TOP
tips

By writing a book pitch you have:

1. Copy for sales brochures.

2. An introduction to your book.

3. Descriptive copy for book retailers and distributors.

4. A brief for cover designer.

5. A brief for editors.

6. A brief for your internal layout.

{

CHAPTER 7

How to speak your first draft

If you are a very slow typist and the thought of handwriting gives you anxiety, speaking and recording your book might be the answer for you.

For some people writing does not come naturally, but speaking and explaining what they do is second nature. If this is you, than recording your first draft may be the difference between publishing a book and just thinking about it.

This chapter looks at the process involved in becoming ready to speak your book, how to turn your recording into a manuscript, and the various tools available.

PREPARATION IS KEY

Before you begin the process, it is important to complete your mind map, outline and book pitch. These will be used to keep you on track while speaking your book.

Ensuring that each of these steps are very detailed, and by including easy to follow bullet points, allows for quick reference while you are speaking. A detailed chapter outline is a great tool for jogging your memory if you come to a blank spot. The clearer you are about what the purpose is of each chapter and section, the easier you will find it to both record your book and stay on track – setting you up for success.

HOW TO TURN THE RECORDING INTO A MANUSCRIPT

Like every phase of the publishing journey, there are choices in how you speak your book and turn it into an editable manuscript. Researching which path you will take will help you decide on the tools you can use to record.

Ways to 'speak your book':

- Speak, then type it out yourself.
- Speak, then have it transcribed.
- Speak your book using an online tool.

Speak, Then Type It Yourself

This option is for those who don't mind typing but find the initial part of getting their thoughts out of their head easier by speaking. Recording can also be a useful tool if you have time away from your writing space that can be used to record. For example: if you are stuck in traffic or waiting for kids at evening training. When inspiration strikes, it is only a matter of pulling out your phone and recording what pops into your head.

Speaking and then typing your manuscript isn't the fastest option but can be a very useful tool for getting information out of your head. This can be especially useful for those in a service industry who spend all day talking to their clients. If you are stuck for what to say, think about what you tell your clients every day.

The major benefit of choosing this option is that it is easy to organise your book after you speak it out because you are typing it up yourself.

Speak, Then Have it Transcribed

This option is the most expensive but can save you hours of time. If you are speaking your book for hours on end, it is recommended that you use a digital recording device to capture everything clearly. This can be a handheld voice recorder, an app on your smartphone, or a program on your computer. It is also beneficial to use a headset with a microphone to ensure what you are saying is clear and cuts out the background noise.

To gain maximum benefit from having your work transcribed, ensure that the recordings are properly organised. It is crucial to hire an experienced and skilled transcriber. If you hire someone with little to no experience, or someone who cannot understand your accent, you will end up having to spend more time and money fixing it up than you would have done doing it yourself in the first place.

Some voice-recording apps to consider are:

Audio Memos App
You can use this app on your smartphone to record your book. It doesn't transcribe your work but can be used to send to a transcriber or to type up yourself.

Smart Voice Recorder
This is a free Android app that provides an automatic and manual sensitivity control for 'skip silence mode' to save time during playback. You can record yourself speaking for long periods of time with no issues.

Speak Your Book Using Online Tools

This option uses dictation software to transcribe your voice and can be very tricky for those new to recording, especially if you don't speak in complete sentences or are not very clear. However, if you have a very structured outline and are clear on what you are writing, this could be a good option for you.

With the continual advancements and changes in technology, this is a constantly updating list. What has been included here is a brief look at what is current at the time of writing, and each varies with ease of use and price.

Dragon Speech Recognition
Dragon Speech is voice recognition software that allows the user to dictate and have their speech transcribed as written text. This is not a free program and there are several options to choose from.

Evernote
Evernote is a free app for managing a variety of different things in an effort to declutter your life. They offer a dictation tool inside their app that lets you speak your notes, which can be very helpful.

Google Docs
Google now offers a completely free service that allows you to speak into your computers internal microphone in Google Docs and it will transcribe as you speak.

Whichever tool you use it is important before you begin to watch a tutorial on how to get the best out of your recording, and having a useable transcription when done. This includes using punctuation as you speak. You do not want to spend hours using speech to text recognition software only to have to spend hours of time putting in punctuation and making sense of what is written. Accuracy is a very important time-saving factor, as it will save you hours of time later in the editing phase.

With all three options, it is best to record your book in segments, chapter by chapter, allowing you to easily break up the recordings and piece them together when you are finished.

If you are speaking your book in its entirety it is important to set daily goals. Set a daily recording limit, experiment a bit in the initial stages and see how many words you record in an hour. This time will depend on how easy you find it to talk your book and how much stopping and starting you do during the recording time. As with writing, the more you practise the easier it will become.

You will have times of the day that you find it easier to record your book, this may be first thing in the morning or during the day. It is probably not a good idea to leave this until after dinner and you have to put the kids to bed. A clear head is needed to produce a quality product that doesn't require hours of work to turn the recording into an editable manuscript.

Define where you are going to record your book and let your family, friends and work colleagues know that this is what you are doing. If you are recording in the office, let your staff know that this is time that you are not to be disturbed. Let your family know that this is your time and they are not to bother you.

Speaking your book isn't for everyone, but some people swear by it.

TOP
tips

1. Be organised.

2. Have a very clear and detailed structure of each chapter before you begin.

3. Research and understand different recording tools.

4. Set daily recording goals.

5. Have a defined recording space.

SECTION TWO

{ How to turn your manuscript
into a published book }

CHAPTER 8

Traditional, self-publishing or swimming with the sharks

You are now at the stage where your book is written, or you are in the process of writing, and the time has come to commence your journey to becoming a published author.

At the outset the writing seemed like the difficult part, but often the production process and marketing is where the challenge begins. It is said that, 'You don't know, what you don't know', and this is certainly the case with publishing and the terminology used.

This chapter looks at the four paths that can be taken to become a published author. You can either publish with a 'traditional publisher', use a 'vanity publisher' or self-publish with an author service provider, or do it all yourself – each has its own challenges.

TRADITIONAL PUBLISHING

I would like to make it clear from the outset that in no way am I dismissing traditional publishers. The vast majority of our clients are traditional publishers and they still have a significant and vital role to play in publishing.

Being published by a traditional publisher is the dream for many authors – signing a contract with a major publisher such as Pan

Macmillan, HarperCollins, Penguin Random House, University Presses ... the list goes on. Although, if you are writing a nonfiction business book this might not be an option as the cons may far out way the pros.

However, if this is your dream and goal, obtaining the elusive deal can be easier said than done. If you're pitching to the larger publishers, you may need to pitch to an agent first, and if the agent takes on your manuscript they will pitch it to the publishers on your behalf.

Whether you are pitching to an agent or directly to the publisher, rejections and waiting for responses are part of the process. The key to having your manuscript even looked at is to ensure you always research the submission guidelines set out by each individual agent and publisher. They all have different requirements and receive hundreds of submissions. If you do not follow these precise requirements, your manuscript (in all likelihood) will not be looked at.

The credibility and validation of having a book deal with a major publisher brings plenty of prestige. The one great advantage of a traditional publisher is their distribution to physical bookstores, airports and other retail outlets.

You will also have access to a team of professionals, including editors, cover designers, layout designers, and a production and marketing team, who will work on bringing your manuscript to life.

However, these benefits need to be weighed up against the cons. It can take a long time to go from finishing your manuscript, to signing a contract, to having a published book.

Using a traditional publisher also means you lose a degree of control – you can have input into the cover, blurb, timing and price, but ultimately this will be the publisher's decision.

You may dream of that large advance and royalty cheque but in reality it is unlikely, especially if you are an emerging author. If you do receive an advance it may take years before you receive any royalties. You will also have to buy your own books, receiving a slight discount off the recommended retail price.

Traditional publishers will promote your book to the bookstores and their distributors for a limited time, but as the author you need to be prepared to market your book to your readers.

VANITY PUBLISHING

A clear distinction should be drawn between 'vanity publishing' and 'self-publishing', where the author finances the publishing of their own book. People often think of companies offering author services as being Vanity Publishers, but this is not the case.

A vanity press may assert rights to published work and have continued fees/royalties on on-going book sales. There are some reputable companies offering this service very successfully, and it is working for the benefit of both the publisher and the author.

Publishing is a highly competitive industry, and unfortunately where there is great want, there are people who will take advantage of that financial want. Vanity publishing will often be expensive and often doesn't deliver on promises made. It is often hard to detect whether any effort has been made to promote and sell your book, which can be a real problem.

These companies exist on the fees paid to them by authors and have little to no interest in the quality of the book or in helping an author market and distribute their work. It is genuinely difficult to market an unknown author, but they will often 'con' unsuspecting authors into believing they will be made famous. By the time an author realises that this is not the case, a contract has been signed and money has been handed over.

Using NSW Fair Trading's 'things to watch out for' as a starting point, the ASA (Australian Society of Authors) has put together a list of warning signs that should alert you to the presence of a vanity publisher.

Warning signs:

- They may require you to pay for 'submission guidelines'.
- They may require you to use – and pay for – their manuscript assessment service before submitting your manuscript.
- They insist that they will only publish work that has 'merit'.
- They praise your work (this one can be hard to ignore).
- They charge inflated prices to publish and 'market' your book.
- They require you to sign a 'non-disclosure agreement' (which means you can't get advice about the contract).
- They offer you a 50% share of net profits (and 50% of nothing is still nothing).
- When the book is not published on schedule, they will give you a string of excuses for the delay.
- They are unlikely to get your book reviewed in any literary journal or major newspaper.
- They will not get your book into bookshops, and online sales will prove elusive.

If you are in any doubt as to whether you are dealing with a vanity publisher, contact the ASA or your local Writers Centre.

- www.nsw.org.au
- www.asauthors.org
- www.qwc.asn.au

The simple way of looking at it is – if you are paying the full costs to produce and publish your book, you should retain all rights, earn all profits and have no on-going fees. If on-going marketing and promotion is offered, do your research on other books they have published and see how well they have sold. This can easily be done by researching on any of the online book distributors, including Amazon. If you find it difficult to locate any of their books, this should answer your question.

Many people have the dream of becoming a published author, but few of us take that step to write and publish. It can be a confusing and frustrating path but it needn't be if you do your research and have a clear set of plans drawn up.

As an entrepreneur, you are independent and are used to doing things on your own time schedule and backing yourself. This is the same with self-publishing.

As with any business, we soon learn that doing it all ourselves is often not the best way to do it, and bringing in an expert saves both time and money.

SELF-PUBLISHING USING AUTHOR SERVICES

Not using a traditional publisher is a developing phenomenon, and it has opened up the market to new authors and seen the expanse of business owners writing a nonfiction book to share their industry knowledge and experience.

The benefit of self-publishing is that it allows authors to manage the production of their work in print, an ebook or both. There are many stages in the self-publishing journey and these include editing, design, production, promotion, selling and distribution, and this is where the confusion begins.

Not so many years ago, self-publishing was frowned upon and seen as unprofessional; however, that view is rapidly changing. Yes, there are self-published books that are unprofessional and look and feel amateurish, but there are ways to achieve the look and quality of a traditionally published book as an independent (indie) author.

The good and the bad news with self-publishing is that you have complete control, and with that comes a lot of responsibility. There is a wealth of author services, freelance editors and designers available to assist you, and often the trick is to pinpoint your strengths and weaknesses and know what services you will find valuable.

The key to working with a business that provides author services, whether that is an individual editor or designer, or a company providing a one-stop solution, is research.

Look at their previous work. If you have enjoyed reading a book, look at the imprint page and see if the editor and cover designer have been listed on the imprint page. Talk to other authors about who they have used and would recommend. Most people are happy to share their experiences, both good and bad, and if you reach out on social media business groups you are bound to receive a few recommendations.

But don't just leave it there, see if you can get hold of their book and double check there standards are equal to yours. What one person is happy with another may consider unprofessional.

Join your local writers centre or an Alli (The Alliance of Independent Authors), which is an international not-for-profit looking out for indie authors. I am an approved service provider.

If you choose to work with several independent people, your time-line may appear something like this:

Manuscript to editor for structural edit	1 July
First draft back from the editor	31 July
Detailed cover brief and a few chapters to cover designer	1 August
Re-edit manuscript and resupply to editor	15 August
Second draft and copyedit back from editor	30 August
First draft of cover design back from designer	1 September

Final edit of manuscript by you completed	15 September
Manuscript to proofreader	15 September
Engage typesetting company to typeset manuscript	15 September
Cover design back and approved	30 September
Supply completed manuscript to typesetter	30 September

As you can see, the key to using a variety of author services is coordination of dates. I recommend using a spreadsheet, and calculate the amount of time required depending on the individual's timeframe. Each will vary depending on how busy they are and how quickly they can turn work around.

Working with an author provider service (a one-stop-shop) will take this stress away, as their role is to coordinate these stages for you. They should ask you your proposed book launch date and commit to whether or not they can work with you to meet your deadlines. If you have a very short turnaround time and require a full edit and cover design, be wary of anyone saying they can do it and still provide a professional job. Remember not all editors are great at editing books.

A one-stop-shop will also be able to provide print ready files to send to your printer or have books printed for you, as well as prepare your files for digital publication. And, depending on the services offered, they can upload your files to your chosen distributors.

No matter which way you choose to go, either employing individuals or a one-stop-shop, do your research and get a variety of quotes, remembering to check they have worked on books before.

SELF-PUBLISHING – DOING IT ALL YOURSELF

While it is possible to self-publish a book completely on your own, it is not a path I would generally recommend. Very few people are talented across all areas of publishing, and in all likelihood you will end up publishing an unprofessional book. A book that screams amateur will be no benefit to either yourself or your business, in fact it could do you more harm than good.

But if this is your only option, due to budget or time, I recommend getting a team of beta readers together who are happy to read your manuscript and offer feedback on the structure, grammar and spelling.

Research covers and don't try and go for anything too complicated, keep it simple. Using free stock photos on your cover will scream self-published book. Research internal layouts of books and take notice of what you like and don't like, look at the running heads, where the page numbers are placed on the page, chapter headings and so on. These are all discussed further in Chapter 11.

It is not impossible to self-publish a professional book on your own, but it is difficult. If budget is tight but can be stretched, I would highly recommending working with an editor and cover designer at the very least.

TOP
tips

1. Research and choose your preferred publishing method.

2. If choosing the traditional publishing journey, research and follow submission guidelines and be realistic about time frames.

3. If self-publishing determine your strengths and weaknesses and define your team accordingly.

4. Whoever you work with research their previous books.

5. If going it alone seek help and advice wherever possible.

6. Don't sign anything without doing your homework.

{ **CHAPTER 9**
The importance of a great editor

Working with an editor for the first time can be a daunting prospect. It is at this time that you face a great many of your fears. However, don't be scared, as it can, and should, be a rewarding experience that will enhance your work, ensuring your voice is heard in the best way possible.

Few people can edit their own work effectively. Authors can have difficulty in foreseeing the message readers interpret from their work. Often what makes sense to you, the author, because of jargon, prior knowledge etc. does not make sense to the reader.

No matter how confident you are with your spelling, punctuation and grammar, an edit is extremely beneficial if you want your work to be polished and professional for all to read and enjoy.

This chapter looks at the different phases of editing, the benefits of using a professional editor, what an editor doesn't do, and what to look out for when researching different editors.

FIRST PHASE OF EDITING: THE SELF-EDIT

There is no right or wrong way to begin the self-editing phase. It can be helpful after you have written your first draft to print everything out and read through it editing it by hand. This is the time that the red pen comes out and gets put to good use.

After the initial edits have been taken in, find a quiet corner and read your manuscript aloud. Reading aloud means you can pick up inconsistencies or sentences that don't flow. It is amazing how many times you can reread something and miss a mistake – reading aloud changes how you process the information on the page.

SECOND PHASE OF EDITING: WORKING WITH A PROFESSIONAL

How many times have you heard someone say, 'I am a grammar Nazi and I can edit my own work'? Only to then read their book and realise no matter how proficient they think they are, there are errors and other inconsistencies.

An editor's role is all encompassing, and depending on your level of writing experience and what style of book you are writing, there are many aspects to determine what editorial package you require.

Over the past decade, while working with editors at some of Australia's largest publishing houses, we have learnt that even our favourite authors of both fiction and nonfiction work very closely with their editor. We see this in the number of author and editor corrections that get taken in after first pages have been formatted. It is not uncommon to get up to a third and fourth round of corrections, and on the rare occasion we have been at the 11th round.

This is not a negative reflection on either the editor or the author; it just shows that every writer benefits immensely from this close working collaboration. Ultimately, it is the reader that gains the greatest benefit from this by having a far superior book to read.

The editing process can at first seem brutal, but it will help your book reach its full potential. Most readers don't realise that all great books have been edited in some form or other. And it's not just a process of inserting a few commas here and there, and checking spelling and grammar. While this is an important step in the editing journey, it is only part of the process, as a lot more is involved.

Authors will sometimes argue the benefits and point of working with an editor, thinking that they don't need one. They feel that their book is already good, not realising that an editor can help turn a *good* book into a *great* book.

Some of the reasons for not using an editor we hear are:

- My husband's an English teacher and he has edited my book.
- Mum reads all day and is a great speller. She has edited my book.
- I was an A grade student in English at high school, I don't need an editor.

While these are all valid reasons to have someone else look over your first draft, they are not good reasons to skip paying for an editor. An English teacher is not an editor and your mother, no matter how much she loves you, will not give you sound professional advice.

If Matthew Condon, Di Morrissey and Matthew Reilly all concede the benefit of working with their editor, and they write full time for a living, there must be value in the process. Even a professional editor understands the value of working with another editor when working on his or her own work.

There are many online forums and websites proclaiming that it is possible to produce and publish a book for a minimal cost – self-editing, designing the cover and internal layout yourself. While this is possible, it is unlikely you will produce a quality professional book.

Your book reflects you and your business. Producing an amateur book that screams self-edited will not be a positive reflection of you as a business professional. It may well harm your credibility, as your readers perceive your lack of value in your own work.

THE EDITOR'S ROLE

It can be a daunting task handing your first draft to your editor, but don't be nervous. Your English teacher back at high school is not grading you. This was how I felt, but I was very reassured by the process and by how much my editor was passionate about helping produce the best work possible.

The editor's role is to walk with you on the editing journey from woe to go. Your editor will correct spelling mistakes, inconsistencies (for example: using past and present tense), grammar mistakes and other errors. A good editor will also:

- Suggest additions if a subject requires clarification or needs more detail.
- Suggest reworking areas where too much industry jargon has been used, especially if your reader is not an industry expert.
- Suggest deletions if you have waffled on for too long on a certain topic.
- Bring your attention to any copyright concerns.
- Suggest ways in which your writing can be improved, for example: you may have a tendency to use a particular word on a regular basis. A good editor will point this out and suggest alternatives.
- Ensure that your text has been styled appropriately for the typesetter.

As you are a self-publishing author, you have the choice as to whether or not you choose to include the editor's decisions. In most cases, I would recommend you listen to the editor. If you are really unhappy with a suggestion, bring the matter up and discuss why you have written something a certain way. Perhaps you can then find a more agreeable solution.

If you are working with a traditional publisher, the publisher and editor will usually have the final say, especially if you are an emerging author. But in our experience, it is usually a very collaborative approach where there may be toing and froing, but the outcome is mostly agreeable.

WHAT'S NOT AN EDITOR'S ROLE?

The role of your editor is not to check your facts. As the self-publisher, this responsibility lies firmly on your shoulders. If writing a book about compliance, engineering or any other topic that requires precise facts, it is your responsibility to do your homework and know that what you have written is correct. A trusted colleague may be a good place to start in verifying your facts are true and correct.

You can pay a specialist editor to do this, but it will be more expensive and most probably take a fair amount of time.

There is nothing worse than proclaiming to be an expert in your field and not fact-checking what you have written. Don't just make stuff up to fill the page. If you are not already an expert in one area, research, research, research.

TYPES OF EDITING
Manuscript Assessment (Substantive/Structural Edit)
A manuscript assessment is the first editorial check you should have, particularly if you are writing a fiction novel.

An editor carrying out an assessment will read through your completed manuscript and focus on the overall structure, content and style of your manuscript. They will look specifically at your narrative, writing style and voice, readability, appropriateness, flow, paragraph styles, inconsistencies, length and presentation.

The editor will provide a thorough review of the above aspects, as well as provide examples and suggestions for improvements. They will be able to demonstrate how grammar, spelling and punctuation may need to be corrected; however, they will not correct these errors in this edit.

A manuscript assessment will give you professional advice on the big overall aspects of your work. It will allow you to see what is working in your manuscript, and what needs to be reworked to ensure you are completely happy with it before handing it over to be copyedited, and to have all errors corrected.

Many writers use a manuscript assessment to make sure that they are on the right track with their writing and that they are fulfilling the objects they set out for themselves when they began to write.

Structural Edit

A structural edit is similar to the manuscript assessment in that the editor looks at the 'big picture' aspects of your manuscript, which concern the structure, voice, flow and clarity of your text. However, in a manuscript assessment, 'suggestions' will be made as to how you can improve these aspects, but no changes will be carried out for you. It will be up to you to do these 'edits' as suggested.

In the structural edit, the editor will actually correct all of these aspects for you, move text around to make it more readable, fix any flow issues, and clarify any sentences, paragraphs, thoughts and ideas for you. They will demonstrate how your text can be reworked for the benefit of your manuscript. By doing this, your manuscript will be another step closer to being 'edited'.

Copyedit

A copyedit ensures that nothing disturbs the interaction between author and reader. Points that are checked and corrected during this edit include:

- Overall structure.
- Clarity of content.
- Narrative, writing style and voice, readability, appropriateness, flow, paragraph styles, inconsistencies, length and presentation.
- Grammar, spelling and punctuation.
- Correct illustrations suitably placed and captioned.
- Completeness and text styled ready for the typesetter.
- Coordination of copyright applications and acknowledgements, legal concerns etc.
- Title page, imprint page, references, indexes, chapters etc. are all complete.

This edit is the most thorough of all edits, and is therefore the most expensive.

WHAT HAPPENS NEXT?

After the editor has finished a round of editing, the marked corrections are sent back to you to go through and decide what changes you are making. If the editor suggests that certain areas of your book do not flow well, now is the time to rewrite these areas.

It can be hard to take what can seem like criticism when you have worked so hard on your book, but this is the time to remember the editor's role is to help you produce a great book that you will be proud of. In the long term, when you are handing over your book to people you admire and want to work with, you will be very pleased that you worked with a professional.

A good way to learn from the editing process is when the marked-up pages with suggestions and corrections are received go through each one and physically take these into your manuscript. This will allow you to become aware of any weaknesses that you do have in your writing. This means that when you come to write your second book, your writing will have improved due to what you learnt from the editing process.

PROOFREADING

Proofreading is the final stage of the editing process. It is best done by someone who has never seen your book before, so uses a fresh set of eyes. It is amazing how many times you can read something and miss a mistake. We tend to read what we want to read and a few sets of eyes will pick up tiny things that have been missed.

HOW TO FIND THE RIGHT EDITOR

Finding the right editor, or author service provider, to work with is an important step in the publishing journey, as you will be working with them closely over a period of weeks or possibly months.

Whether you are working with an editor directly or as part of a self-publishing package, it is important that they are highly skilled and understand the 'why' of your book and what it is that you aim to produce.

Getting referrals from other authors can be a great place to start. Speak to the editor and try to meet face-to-face if possible. Generally, they will ask to see a copy of your manuscript, both to give you a quote and to see if you are a good fit for each other.

Read other books that they have edited, this will give you an idea of how skilled they are as an editor. It may not be a genre similar to your book but it will give you an indication of their skill. Not every editor is as skilled as they proclaim to be.

Ask for a written quote outlining exactly what you will receive, what type of edit, how many rounds of corrections and the time frame. There is nothing worse than choosing an editor only to find out that they cannot begin working on your manuscript for the next

6 to 12 months. Be up front about your planned launch date and what your expectations are.

TIMEFRAMES

The time it takes to edit your manuscript will depend on a variety of factors:

- Manuscript length (word count)
- Genre
- Structure of your book
- Editor's work load

If your book is structured as a 'step-by-step formula' or 'seven reasons to', it is unlikely to have too many problems around flow; however, a manuscript that tells a story can have a narrative that does not flow well. In this case the editing can take longer. At the time of the quote, after the editor has had a look at your manuscript, they should be able to give you a timeframe.

Generally, allow at least four weeks for the first round of editing. For a nonfiction 35,000 to 50,000 word manuscript, two months should usually be enough time to get your manuscript ready to be formatted.

If you are on a tight deadline, corrections can be taken into the formatted book. It will be slightly more expensive but can save time.

COST

Using the 35,000 to 50,000-word manuscript as a guide, you can expect to pay the following:

Manuscript Assessment	$750 to $1200
Developmental Edit	$1500 to $3500

Copyedit	$1500 to $3500
Proofread	$500 to $1000

These figures are only a guide, as like anything prices can vary greatly. If you find an editor who is extremely cheap, thoroughly research them. Using someone who is cheap may end up costing you more in the long term, both financially and with time.

Working with a professional editor should be a great experience that brings you that much closer to your book launch and realising your dream of becoming a published author. You may well experience some ups and downs, and question from time to time why you are doing this, but remember the editing process will take your book from what is potentially a *good* book to a *great* book.

TOP
tips

1. Self-edit your first draft using a red pen.

2. Research editors, ask other authors, read books they have edited.

3. Understand what is and isn't an editor's role.

4. Decide on the type of edit you require.

5. Decide on a workable timeframe.

6. Ask for detailed quotes.

7. Employ a proofreader.

When I asked my own editor, Michele Perry from Wordplay Editing Services, 'Why is an editor's role so important?' she said:

> *An editor's main role is to make their writer's text everything the writer dreamed it could be, and more! They should understand the writer's 'why' and their target audience, and ensure that the book that they write successfully fulfils their goals. Once they understand the writer's ideals they then can put themselves in the reader's shoes and do all they can to make sure that everything written is correct, clear, readable, and most importantly, that the writer's 'voice' is truly represented. Editors not only 'correct' everything, they also help inspire, support, encourage and show a writer how they can make their words truly shine!*

– Michele Perry

{ **CHAPTER 10**
Why a great cover sells copies

The reality is a book is judged by its cover and can make or break a book. This is a stage in the publishing process you do not want to rush.

As a self-publisher, the good and the bad news is you have total control of your cover design. In one quick glance, it needs to tell the story of your book, it is the window into the soul of your book. You want to be able to hand your book over to someone you respect and admire, and feel proud of your book. You do not want to feel embarrassed by a poor-quality cover.

The psychology of the book cover is it is giving people an essence of what they are buying – is your book professional; are you credible? The cover is one of your best tools in your marketing arsenal but can also be something that goes horribly wrong.

This chapter looks at the different styles of book covers, why a great cover is important, questions to ask your designer, and the stages in the design process.

THE COVER AS A WHOLE

The front cover is only one aspect of your book cover. When designing your cover, the front, back and spine should be viewed as a whole and need to flow as a consistent design.

The front cover grabs the reader's attention and is often the first thing they will look at. Imagine yourself in a bookstore, what do you do? You pick up a book, look at the cover and turn it over and read the blurb.

The back cover should not be an afterthought and needs to be carefully planned. It has a great impact and can be what clinches the sale. More detail about what should be included on your back cover is discussed in Chapter 12.

If the reader is still not convinced, they might look at the spine and the first few pages, perhaps even the contents page.

How many times have you looked at a book in a bookstore and not bought it because there was just something not quite right about the cover? Getting the cover right requires a specialist who has designed covers in the past and is usually not the same designer who does your internal layout.

INITIAL DESIGN PHASE: RESEARCH

What makes a great cover is terribly subjective and differs from genre to genre. Elements like image, font face, featured characters, and colours all impact the emotional reaction of your potential reader.

Like fashion, book covers go through trends and the themes change. These include covers based on photos, scripted fonts, illustrated and font only.

You may think that this is up to your designer to know what is on trend, but it is important that you have an idea of what is currently selling. Do your research both online and in your local bookstore. Look at your competitor books and take note of what grabs your attention, but more importantly what doesn't. Look at the back covers and read them.

One thing to remember is that your cover needs to be versatile. It should look great both as a printed book and as a thumbnail online. When you find covers that you like in your bookstore, look them up on Amazon and see how effective they are as a thumbnail. You will be surprised by the difference a cover design can have on its visual effect online.

DESIGNING A CONCEPT

Deciding on the message you want to send to potential readers will give you direction when putting together a 'design brief'. Even if you are designing the cover yourself, it is helpful to mind map a design brief as this will help give you clarity on the message you are trying to portray.

Ask yourself, 'What is my target audience looking for?' and 'What is the book's purpose?' Is it – inspiration, how to get from here to there, or is it about success and achievement?

Narrowing this concept down will help you come up with ideas and visual metaphors that in turn will help determine the imagery, choice of colours, typography and layout. These design concepts will assist in portraying the message of the book.

There are three types of covers that are used and they are:

- Photographic, for example:
  Never Stop Believing, Sally Obermeder
- Text only, for example:
  7 *Habits of Highly Effective People,* Stephen Covey
- Illustrated, for example:
  When Michael Met Mina, Randa Abdet Fattah

There is no right or wrong when it comes to choosing a concept, it is a personal choice. A 'text only' cover can be hard to get right, and 'illustrated' covers are very contemporary at the moment as they are a bit more creative. Ensure you research the market to see what is current and what you like.

Don't rush this stage of working on a concept design. If you start feeling overwhelmed, close your eyes and imagine giving your book to someone you respect and feel that overwhelming sense of pride. How good does that feel?

GENRE IS IMPORTANT

The book cover should reflect the genre of the book. A great book cover 'talks' to your readers through the use of imagery, typography and colours. When looking at your cover, the reader should get a sense of what they will get from reading your book.

A good cover for a nonfiction book should communicate the tone of the book. A cover for a law book will be very different to a book on mindfulness. Thorough research in your genre will help narrow this down.

GETTING IT WRONG

When thinking about your cover design it is good practice to look at bad design examples. Pinterest is a great place to start. Overwrought and over-thought typography is a frequent offender, and stock imagery can ruin a book's visual credibility. A poorly designed cover is a signal that your book is self-published, and people will look at your cover and make an instant decision based on it.

BACK COVER DESIGN

As mentioned earlier, your back cover is an important piece of the cover design – it can be the piece that closes the sale.

Your back cover blurb should clearly clarify who your book is written for, what the problem is you are solving, and what value the reader will get from reading your book. The reader isn't just investing their money in your book, they are also investing their time. Why should they make such an investment with you? Your blurb is the best opportunity you have to make this sale.

Other important things to include are:

- Quote or testimonials from an influential thought leader.
- Great author photo – you are selling yourself and your business, and a great photo is a wonderful way to allow readers to begin a relationship with you.
- Recommended Retail Price (RRP).
- Barcode, including ISBN.
- Call to action.

Take the time to invest in researching competitors' back covers. What information calls you to buy and read their books?

Authors often say that the back cover blurb can be the hardest part of the book to write, so don't leave this to the last minute to write. Spend time writing a few different versions and ask for feedback from your network.

BOOK SPINE

Why is the book spine important? Glance up and look at your book-shelf, what do you see? Only the books' spines! This is the same in most bookstores. Unless you are a bestseller, getting prominent placing on front shelves, the most a potential reader will see is your book spine.

A good book spine will include:

- Book title.
- Author Name.
- Publishers Logo, this could be your business logo.

Self-published authors often forget to include a logo on the bottom of the book spine. If you look at your bookshelf you will notice that all traditionally published books include the publisher's logo. Most readers don't consciously notice this, but they do if it is missing. This one exclusion can be what makes your book look self-published.

CHOOSING A COVER DESIGNER OR AUTHOR SERVICE PROVIDER

When looking for a cover designer it is important to work with someone who has experience designing book covers. Not all graphic designers have this experience.

Shop around and ask for recommendations from any authors whom you know.

When conducting your research look at the imprint pages of books you like and the cover designer will be mentioned here. In some cases the designer will be a freelancer and you can go directly to them.

If you are working with an author service provider, ask about their cover designer. Some will use an in-house designer, others will work with freelancers or a combination of both. What follows applies to both working directly with the designer or an author service provider.

Points to Consider When Engaging a Designer

1. *What covers have you designed in my genre?* It is important to get a sense of the work the designer has in your genre. You may want to work with a designer who has worked in your genre, as they will have an understanding of what works well and what is currently on trend. Like fashion, cover design changes with time, and what resonated with readers a few years ago may not be the case now. While it is not out of the ordinary for a designer to work across multitudes of genres, it is important that they have

a process for researching your genre to gain an understanding of what readers expect.

2. *Define your concept design.* While we would like our cover designer to be able to read our minds, unfortunately this is not usually the case. To ensure you are on the same page it is important that you come up with a concept. When engaging a cover designer, they will give you a document to fill out and more than likely ask for the manuscript, your book pitch or a few chapters to read.

3. *Consider your creative brief.* Be as clear as possible in articulating what the desired outcome is. A great cover designer will be able to listen to and understand your brief to come up with a cover that suits your content. They will have different ideas to you, but should be willing to listen to you and try and gauge a sense of what you want. It can be a bit like working with an editor, you may not agree on everything but you should be able to come to an agreeable outcome.

4. *Research your genre across a multitude of platforms.* Look online at Amazon and iTunes and see what is selling well. Go to bookstores and take note of what catches your eye and what you dismiss. See if you can see a recurring theme. Do they all have a common thread, use of images, colours and typefaces?

5. *Images.* Depending on your budget and the package that you take, the designer will determine how you go about this. Choosing from an image library is a cost effective way of getting a high quality image for a cover. Bear in mind though that you will not have the sole rights for this image, and you may see it elsewhere. If this isn't something you want to risk, you can either commission a photoshoot or your designer can create a custom artwork for your sole use. This can significantly increase the cost, and not all designers offer this service. Something to consider when having

an image designed is to ensure that it captures the essence of your book. It is not a good idea to use a beautiful image created by a family member if it bears no resemblance to your book. No matter how beautiful the artwork, it will not do your book any favours.

6. *Don't rush into a decision.* Getting a cover designed makes the book writing process seem real. You are not far from being a published author. But in the excitement, don't rush into picking a cover designer that Aunty Mary suggested, do your research. View their work to see if you like it and to ensure that their style resonates with you. Covers are like art, what appeals to one person may not appeal to another.

7. *Fees and payment structure.* The old saying, 'How long is a piece of string', applies to what a cover designer charges. It can depend on their level of industry experience, awards and if they have worked in the traditional publishing industry. Some have their fee structure on their websites while others provide custom quotes. In Australia, expect to pay anything from $600 to $2000 upwards. You can have covers designed for less using online services such as Upworks and fiverr, but you may not get the same quality of work.

8. *Clarify the design process.* How many versions of the cover will be supplied at the first-round cover stage? Will there be more than one? Will the designer create several variations of the same concept design or will they supply two vastly different designs? How many revisions are included in the cost and are there additional charges for multiple changes? You need to clarify that the designer is happy to work with your feedback.

9. *Obtain an upfront quote.* Ask for a written quote clearly outlining exactly what is included in the cost, such as how many concept designs and revisions are included.

DESIGN PROCESS

While every designer is different, the process will follow something like this:

1. *Initial consultation call.* Now is the time to discuss your genre, ideas and what your book is about. This discussion should also include your timeline and what the designer's working style is.

2. *Quote.* The designer will deliver a quote or you will decide on the package that works for you.

3. *Delivery of brief.* When price has been agreed upon, you will deliver your written design brief, outline your book size, colours etc. If not already supplied, the designer will request your book pitch, as well as your complete manuscript, or a few chapters, to understand your book and its message. At this stage you will clearly define your required dates. Don't be vague, request an exact date. If you have seen covers you like, now is a good time to send copies of these. Send photos or screen shots.

4. *First round concept.* The designer will send you some concepts of what they think the cover will look like. They probably won't be polished, as they are to be used as a tool for feedback to ensure they are headed in the right direction. Depending on the designer and the initial agreement, you may receive several first cover concept designs.

5. *Final concept round.* The designer will send you a final version or the front cover, back cover and spine.

6. *Delivery.* Your designer should supply you with a hi-res JPEG and/or PDF of your final design, including all elements. If you haven't made final decisions on some of the elements i.e. the titles, you many require the photoshop or InDesign file, depending on the program the designer uses. Not all designers are happy to supply these and this needs to be discussed ahead of time.

TESTING POTENTIAL COVERS

Testing potential covers is especially important if you are either unsure of which concept design works best, are using overseas designers, or designing the cover yourself.

There are a number of ways to do this and it will depend on your network, target audience and a multitude of other factors.

Some of the ways to conduct research are:

- Run a poll on your website. A simple tool like Playbuzz can be embedded directly on your website or blog post. You have to rely on your own network of respondents, but if you have an established audience you'll not only get responses from people who would probably buy your book but you are promoting your upcoming book to your potential reader.
- Run an email A/B test campaign.
- Run a survey campaign, either to your network or a paid campaign.
- Run a FaceBook campaign. If you are a member of business groups or groups specialising in your genre, for example: health and wellbeing, create a post featuring your book covers and ask for feedback and preferences. From what I have witnessed, people are generally happy to offer constructive feedback and are genuinely excited for the author and the journey they are undertaking.

Remember, you may not like everything that everyone says, but that is okay. It is better to hear negative feedback before you have paid for printing, and it is always your choice to listen and act on the feedback. The respondents may not be in your target niche and have little understanding of your industry.

Whichever road you choose to design your cover, it is important to remember how much weight the design can have on the overall success of you book. BookBub testing has shown that a cover alone can account for 30 per cent difference in clicks. Thirty per cent of sales is a lot of sales to miss out on and a lot of potential customers who will never get to learn about you and your business.

TOP
tips

1. Research what style of cover you like.

2. Research your competitors' book covers.

3. Spend time writing a great back cover blurb.

4. Include a logo on the book spine.

5. Research cover designers and author service providers.

6. Get a quote including how many concepts and revisions are included.

7. Be clear on the timeframe.

8. Ask for feedback on concept designs.

Over the years we have had the great pleasure of working with the award-winning designer, Sandy Cull, from gogoginko designs. She was the cover designer for this book. As to what makes a great book cover Sandy says:

A great book cover design attracts readers to the book, such that they choose yours before all the others near and next to it.

A great book cover should be not only true to the text within, but unique to it. It should capture the entire narrative in one fabulous visual: a visual that is compelling and unexpected. It needs to be immediately eye-catching, and a little surprising. In order to achieve these things, the designer needs to understand the words within. This requires reading the manuscript, not only to find its visual cues, but to achieve an understanding of its themes and ideas. The best covers for 'Animal Farm' show something far more complex and interesting than just the animals.

Unfortunately, publishers and designers are often restrained by the dictates of the market where there is pressure to cover a book with the safest, 'proven', familiar approach. This means there are a lot of covers that look the same. Though it can seem counter intuitive, taking risks visually is a more intelligent and clever approach. Covers that are doing something new will be noticed and memorable and intriguing. Taking risks will sell more books. Ironically, the more famous the author, the less creative and courageous and interesting the cover will be.

There are no rules about the size of the type or whether a font should be sans serif or serif. There are no rules about an image being better black and white or coloured, illustrative or photographic. These things are determined by the most important thing, the words within, and are tailored individually on a book-by-book basis.

– Sandy Cull

CHAPTER 11
Great layout says professional book

The internal layout of your book is as equally important as having a great cover and professionally edited book. A lot of self-published books have awful internal layouts and this reflects badly on both you, as the author, and your business.

This is a very easy step to overlook as you have seen and read hundreds of books, how hard can it be? Believe it or not, designing a great internal layout is harder than it seems and should not be done by a graphic designer who has never worked on books before.

This chapter looks at all the aspects that make up a good internal layout and what to avoid.

WHY IS IT SO IMPORTANT?

The aim of a great layout is for it to make reading your book easy, and it should be something the reader doesn't even notice. Generally, a reader will only notice the internal layout if they are in the industry or if it is amateurish. If the reader thinks your book looks 'not quite right', they will think you and your business are 'not quite right'.

Trends in internal layout, like cover design, change over time. In the past there was a tendency to use a smaller font and crowd the page, using very little white space. This was because printing was more expensive than it is today and putting more words on a page saved pages and therefore costs.

Knowing what to avoid in internal layout is probably the easiest and clearest way of working out what you need to consider:

- Text (copy) too big or too small.
- Text bunched together and crowded.
- No white space, no spare pages between sections.
- Missing information in the prelims.
- Lack of consistency, using different fonts, running heads etc.
- Using too many fonts or difficult to read fonts.
- Inappropriate layout, wrong style for the book, using a document style.
- Using inappropriate images, irrelevant or lo-res and poor quality.

ASPECTS TO CONSIDER

What follows is a brief explanation of each of the aspects to consider when working with your designer and typesetter. When you are reading books look out for these design elements to help distinguish what appeals to you. You may be surprised by the elements on a page that you have never noticed before.

Text on the Page

When you are considering your internal layout, your designer or type-setter will ask you a number of questions and one will be about the type size. This refers to the size of the type and the distance between the baseline of one line to the next. This is explained in more detail in the glossary.

Using a type size that is either too big or too small will look amateurish and cheap. Using a type size that is too small makes reading your book difficult and an unenjoyable experience.

White Space

White space is used in the internal design to enhance the reader's experience. This is taken into account when considering the gutters and margins on a page and the layout of chapters and sections.

Often in business books, white space – spare pages – will be inserted to define sections, chapters may always start on a right-hand page (recto page) and inclusions of tips or quotes can be designed on their own page.

Prelims

The correct layout of your prelims is an extremely important step in ensuring you produce a professional book. Look at the books on your bookshelf and you will notice they all have a similar layout in the beginning of the book and will include these items:

- Title Page
- Imprint Page
- Dedication
- Contents
- Acknowledgments
- About the Author
- Testimonials

You do not have to include all these pages, but it is a good idea to include most. Skipping these and going straight into your story will have you presenting a dodgy-looking book, and nobody wants that.

Title Page

When your cover designer has completed the cover, ask them to produce a black and white version to be used as your title page. This will use the same fonts as your cover and include the book title, author name and publisher, and it will tie-in nicely with the cover.

Imprint Page

The imprint page, or copyright page, is usually on the back of the title page on the verso (the left-hand page). You don't have to reinvent the wheel with the imprint page, simply copy one imprint page from another book. It should include – the copyright notice, ISBN, publisher, type and font used, cover designer, and typesetter.

Dedication

This is a personal choice and is more often seen in works of fiction, but if there is someone you would like to dedicate your book to this is where you would do it.

Acknowledgement

An acknowledgement page can be at the front or back of the book – my personal preference is at the front of the book. This is a nice page to write as you get to mention people and thank them.

You don't want to write ten pages thanking everyone from your primary school teacher to the dog, but including those who have genuinely helped you is a lovely way to say thank you. Most people get a real kick out of having their name in print and it is a really special way to acknowledge people. A good guide as to how long this should be is one to two pages long.

About the Author

The 'About the Author' page should be a short one-page synopsis about you and can go at the front or back of the book. For a work of nonfiction, I prefer to have the 'About the Author' page at the front of the book. It helps establish credibility and allows the reader to gain an insight into who you are and why they should read your book.

Fonts and Typefaces

Fonts and typefaces are one of those things we give little or no thought to in our everyday lives. They surround us daily – on street signs, billboards, movie posters, books, newspapers, sides of trucks, and just about everything else we buy.

Typefaces are now over 560 years old, but until about 25 years ago we barely knew their names. The everyday access to computers and the pull-down font menu has made us aware of the vast array of different fonts available.

Growing up in the seventies and eighties before paid TV and the Internet, you would wait with anticipation for your favourite TV shows. In my case this was heightened even further because we lived in the country and only had access to the ABC, so visiting family in the big smoke of Toowoomba meant we could view commercial television. Oh, the heady sense of excitement this brought us kids. As we sat glued to the TV our sense of anticipation grew as the opening credits progressed and the theme song took hold. Maybe, not always the 'greatest' typography or 'classic' design, the font choices used for TV shows were brilliant at being memorable. You only have to look at *I Love Lucy*, *Batman*, *Mash*, *Monty Python*, *Gilligan's Island* and *The Brady Bunch* and you are instantly taken back to another era.

THE INFLUENCE OF STEVE JOBS

After one paid semester at University in 1972, Jobs spent 18 months hanging out at Reed University studying Calligraphy. His professor was the ex-trappist Monk, Robert Pallandio.

Jobs not only learnt about serif and sans serif typefaces, but the varying amount of space between different letter combinations and what makes great typography. It was during this time that Jobs not only picked up calligraphy skills but a certain mindset about typography.

When Jobs designed his first Macintosh computer, it was a machine that came with something unprecedented for this time – a wide range of fonts, including familiar types such as Times New Roman and Helvetica. Jobs also introduced new designs, seemingly taking great care in their appearance and naming. They were named after cities he loved such as Chicago and Toronto.

His desire was for each of them to be as distinct and beautiful as the calligraphy he had studied a decade earlier. The fonts Venice and Los Angeles were designed with a handwritten look to them.

This was the beginning of the shift to where the everyday person had a relationship with letters and type. Previously, this relationship was the domain of those with a technical knowledge in the design and print trade.

Jobs' fonts are not easy to find these days, as they are coarsely pixelated and cumbersome to manipulate. But in the mid 1980s and early 90s, the ability to change fonts was like technology from a science fiction movie. What would they design next, people questioned. Mobile phones perhaps?

Prior to 1984, all the layman had on offer was the dull typefaces of the manual typewriter. If you were very flash, you had an electric typewriter or a very primitive mainframe computer. In the beginning, Apple used Chicago (not on the drop-down menu any longer) for all its menus and dialogs on screen, right through to the time of the early iPods. IBM and Microsoft would soon follow suit.

Because I had dropped out and didn't have to take the normal classes, I decided to take a calligraphy class to learn how to do this. I learned about serif and san serif typefaces, about varying the amount of space between different letter combinations, about what makes great typography great. It was beautiful, historical, artistically subtle in a way that science can't capture, and I found it fascinating.

None of this had even a hope of any practical application in my life. But ten years later, when we were designing the first Macintosh computer, it all came back to me. And we designed it all into the Mac. It was the first computer with beautiful typography. If I had never dropped in on that single course in college, the Mac would have never had multiple typefaces or proportionally spaced fonts. And since Windows just copied the Mac, it's likely that no personal computer would have them. If I had never dropped out, I would have never dropped in on this calligraphy class, and personal computers might not have the wonderful typography that they do. Of course it was impossible to connect the dots looking forward when I was in college. But it was very, very clear looking backwards ten years later.

Again, you can't connect the dots looking forward; you can only connect them looking backwards. So you have to trust that the dots will somehow connect in your future. You have to trust in something – your gut, destiny, life, karma, whatever. This approach has never let me down, and it has made all the difference in my life.

– Steve Jobs

This was a time that marked a freedom from the physical demands of printing and the frustrations of rubbing a sheet of Letrastet, leading to a change in our relationship with words and our creative expression through playing with word design.

Today there is nothing simpler than pulling down the font menu and choosing a font. What makes us choose one font over another? What impression are we trying to create? What are we really saying?

There are over hundreds of thousands of fonts in the world, so why do we not keep to a dozen or so? Say the familiar ones, Times New Roman, Helvetica, or the classic Garamond, named after the type designer Claude Garamond active in Paris in the first half of the 16th Century.

You only have to walk around your city streets and take notice of all the engaging font choices used, from brands well known that we have grown up with to quirky bars, and see that the diversity of fonts and type is huge. Some assault the senses, while others are a work of art.

Think of classic fonts that have etched a path in our psyche. Think of the Obama campaign that will forever be remembered for the typeface Gotham, or the classic typefaces of the London Underground. They are instantly recognisable, even if you haven't travelled to London.

We live in healthy typographical times – the font is here to stay. Steve Jobs and his digital rivals brought about a world where we are individual masters of type. It's a world where we are more aware of 'fonts' than ever before.

Consistency of Layout

Nothing screams amateur book more than inconsistencies throughout your book. The same font should be used throughout, and if using break-out quotes these should also be in a consistent font and style.

Running heads should be the same throughout the book and folios should be placed consistently in the same place on the page.

Careful attention should be taken with the line spacing between chapter heads and the opening line. Headings also need to be a consistent style and size. Having inconsistencies not only says amateur book but suggests you do not value your book enough to spend the time on getting these things right, therefore why should the reader value your book and what you have to say? Consistency of layout, and the care you take to get it right, is an indication of your credibility.

End Pages

The end of your book is a great place to say thank you to your readers for buying and reading your book. Think about including an inspirational quote that will inspire the reader to take action.

At the conclusion of your book leave a page or two and include a sales page. This should be written in the third person, keeping what you write simple, and include here your website and contact details.

Testimonials

Testimonials are a powerful inclusion and can be at the back or the front of your book. Placing them at the front of your book gives the reader a greater opportunity to discover these if they are still deciding to buy your book. The testimonial should be about *you* not the book.

Testimonials help establish credibility and can be sourced from a range of people who do not have to be celebrities. They do, however, need to be credible and the reader needs to resonate with the words.

The use of powerful testimonials is not limited to your book, you can use one or two on the back cover, on your website, media releases, brochures and anywhere else you have collateral.

Sample Pages

In the initial design phase your typesetter will supply you with at least two sample settings to choose from. Print these out in the actual size of your book and fold them to appear as the finished product. This will not only bring your book closer to 'life', but it will give you a very clear indication if you are happy with the design, font and look of your book.

Terminology

Publishing is full of jargon and terminology, some you will be familiar with, some you will know what it is but not what it is called, and others you will have never heard of. What is a dinkus, an en dash, an orphan or widow? The glossary section of this book includes all the common terms used in publishing and can be used as a guide to answer any questions about the layout of your book.

TOP
tips

1. Don't underestimate the importance of the internal design and layout of your book.

2. Be consistent throughout your book.

3. Choose fonts that are easy to read.

4. Choose a type size that is not too big or too small.

5. Look at other books for industry standard preliminary pages.

6. Where possible get testimonials and include either in the front prelim pages or at the back of your book.

CHAPTER 12

ISBN – What is it you ask? The backend of publishing that needs to be done

There are various factors that need to be taken into account to enable the ease of sale and distribution of your book. Since the 1970s, this has been done on a global scale, therefore allowing for tracking of individual books across multiple territories.

This chapter looks at how this is done, why it is important to obtain ISBNs and barcodes even if you aren't initially intending to sell your book. These may seem like minor items but can be the difference between your book appearing professional or amateur.

WHAT IS AN ISBN?

An ISBN is an International Standard Book Number and identifies the registrant, the title, edition and the format of the book.

In 1970, the ISO Standard was created and they were ten digits in length. As of December 2006, the standard became 13 digits. An ISBN is essentially a unique commercial book identifier used by publishers, booksellers, libraries, internet retailers and anyone else in the supply chain for ordering, listing, sales records and stock control purposes.

WHAT IS THE PURPOSE OF AN ISBN?

As the ISBN is a unique international number it enables easy discovery of your book and is the standardised processing and distribution of books through a global chain. This unique number not only identifies your book, but also each individual format of your book, as each format has its own ISBN. So if you print hardback and paperback versions of your book and sell through a distributor, the unique ISBN allows for easy tracking of your book sales.

DO I NEED AN ISBN?

We always advise that 'yes, you do'. Firstly, if you plan on selling your book through brick and mortar bookshops, other retail outlets or placing in libraries, you most definitely need an ISBN and barcode for the print edition. If you only plan on selling your book digitally, you still require an ISBN for sites such as iBooks and Kobo.

If you are not going to sell your book through these outlets or perhaps plan on giving your book away, you do not require an ISBN. However, we still recommend you have one.

An ISBN looks professional – without one your book looks self-published and this is not the aim when producing a high-quality business book. Unless you have a crystal ball, you cannot predict the future. Who knows how your book will be received? You might change your mind and decide to sell your book and therefore need it to be available to a wider audience.

IS ONE ISBN ENOUGH?

In most circumstances we recommend purchasing three ISBNs. As mentioned above, each format of your book requires a separate ISBN, for example: you need one for the print book, one for the epub file and one for the Amazon (mobi) ebook. Technically you do not need your own ISBN for Amazon, they can assign one for your book, but we do not recommend this and discuss this later in the chapter.

DO YOU REQUIRE A NEW ISBN FOR REPRINTS

A new ISBN needs to be assigned if there are significant changes to any part or parts of a publication. If there are changes to the title, subtitle, or format (size) a new ISBN needs to be assigned. Minor changes, for example corrections to misprints, do not require a separate ISBN.

WHERE TO BUY AN ISBN?

An ISBN is assigned, not created, therefore it is important to purchase one from a reputable source. In Australia, the official agency is Thorpe-Bowker, and authors can purchase online from them or through their self-publishing service provider. They are not expensive but as a one-off purchase you will need to pay a set-up fee with Thorpe-Bowker. This can be avoided by purchasing one through your service provider who will already have a publishing account set up.

ARE ISBNS DISPLAYED ON THE BOOK?

The ISBN must appear on the item itself.

In the case of printed books, the ISBN must appear on the:

- Verso of the title page (copyright page).
- Lower section of the outside back cover.
- Foot of the back of the jacket, or any other protective case or wrapper, if using.

In the case of electronic publications, the ISBN must appear on the:

- Title display, the first display, or on the screen that displays the title or its equivalent.

If a book is being produced in various formats and is available separately, then all ISBNs should be listed one below the other on all versions.

For example:
ISBN 978-586-2344-3 (paperback)
ISBN 978-586-2356-2 (kindle)
ISBN 978-586-2311-5 (epub)

Displaying the ISBNs looks professional and will help ensure your book is taken seriously.

AMAZON EBOOKS

If you upload to Amazon Kindle Direct you do not need an ISBN for this format as Amazon will format your book and allocate an ISBN. We prefer not to do this as you have no control over the outcome. We prefer to format all files with allocated ISBNs prior to uploading to Kindle.

BARCODES

We are all familiar with barcodes and their uses. This code is generated from your ISBN and placed on the back cover of your book. You can buy them from Thorpe-Bowker, or your printer, designer or self-publishing company might provide one. Make sure it is not too small or covered by other material on your back cover. Generally they appear on the bottom right-hand corner of your back cover and display the RRP directly above.

CIP

CiP stands for 'Cataloguing in Publication' and is a service operated by the National Library of Australia to provide a catalogue record for a publication before it is published. The entry includes information such as the title, author, ISBN and subject headings. This information is then put online, making it widely searchable.

CiP is a free service and there is no legal obligation to include a CiP entry in your book. The benefit of the service is that your book's information is widely searchable and routinely used by libraries and the bookselling sector when placing advance orders. This can be useful if you are planning on running a marketing campaign prior to your book launch or hoping to garnish media attention.

It can take up to ten days to process an application – this form is available on the National Library website and you will need to have your ISBN prior to lodging this.

LEGAL DEPOSIT

Legal Deposit is a requirement under the Copyright Act 1968 that has enabled the National Library of Australia to collect Australian publications for more than 100 years. In Australia, it is a legal requirement to deposit a copy of your publication with the National Library of Australia and your State Library. This applies for both offline and online publications. For printed books (offline) a copy of your book should be sent within one month of publication.

At the time of publication the address is:

Legal Deposit

National Library of Australia

Canberra

ACT 2600

A copy should also be sent to your state library. Online copies only need to be provided upon request and must be made available within one month. Publications take 1–2 months to be catalogued and processed, and when your book has been processed you will be able to view it on http://catalogue.nla.gov.au/ and http://trove.nla.gov.au/. The National Library catalogue records have a high visibility in search engine results and are distributed to Worldcat, an international bibliographic database.

The backend of publishing is not at all glamorous and can be somewhat tedious, but all these small steps go towards helping you publish a professional book that the average reader will not be able to differentiate from a traditionally published book.

TOP
tips

1. Decide how many ISBNs you require.

2. Purchase ISBNs.

3. Purchase a barcode.

4. Forward a copy to the Legal Deposit and your state library.

CHAPTER 13

Contracts, copyright and global rights

There has never been a better time for writers to expand and reach out to new markets and new readers, listeners and viewers. The changes in technology have changed the environment for how writers can sell their rights. This makes the process in some ways less complex; however, on the other hand it adds another dimension to what a self-publishing author needs to understand.

'The advent of online global platforms, right down to social media, the internet and email means potential licensers and licensees can engage 24/7, whatever their territory', says Tom Chalmers of IPR License, one of the online platforms facilitating authors in their search for rights for buyers and sellers. With the internet, everyone can know your name and get to know your books.

This expanding market has created its own challenges and has opened up risks for writers. There are bad contracts, and authors often don't understand how to protect their rights. The risks are further increased because more authors now work on their own behalf, where in the past, writers would work with a literary agent who would handle all negotiations on their behalf.

Authors have been known to grant a vanity publisher all rights for their work including, print, ebooks, audio, video, films, TV and other subsidiary rights.

In this chapter you will come to understand what a contract should involve, what an author 'owns', and aspects of 'copyright' laws.

UNDERSTAND THE CONTRACT

If you want to be published then you will be signing a contract that involves either selling your rights, or paying distributors or self-publishing service companies an upfront fee or commission.

Traditionally, if you were signing with a publisher you would work with an agent who would negotiate the rights you were selling. Now this has become the role of the author, and most do not have adequate knowledge of contract terminology and inadvertently sign deals that are not in their favour.

For many authors, of any genre, having a publisher express interest in the rights for their work is validation of their book. Contract negotiation is not the time to sit back and relax, now that a publisher has shown interest, as your publishing rights are valuable assets and should be treated as such.

A whole book could be written about 'Publishing Contracts', so I have some suggested reading at the end of the chapter. What follows is a brief overview of copyright and publishing rights. Please note that none of this should be considered 'legal advice', and I would strongly advise getting professional help if you are considering signing any contracts.

WHAT DOES A WRITER OWN?

Author income is derived from the copyright in the created work. Copyright law gives the author the right to control the publication and other exploitation of the work. The author can decide whether to sell those rights, to whom and on what terms. Typically, rights are sold in the form of licenses, and the compensation is in the form of a flat fee or royalties. All authors need to understand the basics of copyright law in order to protect their rights and maximize potential income.

– 'How Authors Sell Publishing Rights'
Helen Sendwick & Orna Ross

'A Book is the author's property, it is the child of his invention, the brat of his brain.' Daniel Defoe.

In the majority of western countries, copyright is created as soon as an author puts the work into a tangible form, whether that is putting pen to paper or typing directly into a computer. Registration is not required, it is automatically created at the time of writing.

Generally, an author's work is subject to the law of the country where they reside or where the work is first published. Currently in Australia, copyright is 70 years but there has been debate in parliament to amend this to 17 years.

There is no international copyright, but due to various treaties an author's copyright is recognised in most countries.

As the copyright holder, you control who uses your property and how they use it. These ways include:

- Reproducing the work in books or other formats.
- Selling, distributing and commercially exploiting the work.
- Creating derivative works, such as translations, adaptations, sequels and abridgements, films, plays, apps.
- Displaying or performing the work publicly, either live or in recorded form.

As with your house or car, your copyright interest may be sold, assigned, licensed, given away, and bequeathed. This can be an important consideration when preparing your legal documents.

I have recently been working with Barbara, helping her publish her late husband's children's books and other work. It was only in his final weeks that legal papers were signed, bequeathing all manuscripts to her. If this hadn't occurred, this would have been left to other family members who did not share his dying wish of seeing his work published.

At the time of writing this book Copyright Law is hotly being contested throughout the world. This is mainly due to the changes in digital technology. The US Authors Guild is currently leading a battle against Google in order to protect the rights of authors. One side argues that writers must be paid for their work, and copyright is the best way to ensure this happens. Others believe copyright infringes the free flow of information, education and inspiration. This is a very complex issue and if you would like to know more, a good place to start is the Electronic Frontier Foundation.

WHAT IS NOT PROTECTED BY COPYRIGHT?

Copyright protection varies from country to country. In Australia, titles, names and short phrases are copyright free. This is why you see similar or the exact same title for very different books.

If you are writing nonfiction, historical fiction, real world facts, and events, these are not protected, anyone can write about those same events, even if you were the first to discover them.

Copyright protects the execution and expression of an idea into a written piece, not the idea itself.

COPYRIGHT MARK

Technically you do not have to include the © but it is a good idea, as it lets the world know you have ownership of your material.

The copyright notice, generally included on the imprint page, includes three parts:

- © or copyright.
- Year of first publication, that is, when it is available to the public.
- Name of the copyright owner. It can be a pen name or the name of an organisation.

Include 'All Rights Reserved' as this is a requirement in some foreign countries. In Europe, another common phrase is – 'The moral rights of the author have been asserted.'

HOW LONG DOES COPYRIGHT LAST?

In Australia, the duration of an author's copyright is 70 years from their death. In the case of posthumously published works, it is 70 years from the date of publication. Copyright can be given away, subdivided, bequeathed, sold, licensed or leased.

WORKING WITH A SELF-PUBLISHING PROVIDER

Unless you are working with an unscrupulous self-publishing service provider, you will not be transferring any rights to them, other than the non-exclusive right to use your work to produce and distribute books on your behalf. This may include the right to display and market your book on their website and social media.

FAIR USE, GAINING PERMISSION

People may use portions of your work for education, commentary or even criticism. Such use can be done without permission of the copyright owner.

How much of a portion can be used and what 'fair use' actually is, is hard to define. To be safe, contact the copyright owner and get their permission. This includes any music lyrics or film scenes, especially those of Disney. Any industry that has a large productised business based on their industry is best to be avoided without gaining written permission.

PUBLISHING RIGHTS

> *The right to produce or reproduce a book in any form – as a reprint, or a movie or in translation – is a publishing right. Publishing rights are granted by an author to a publisher or producer typically in the form of a licence (permission to use). A successful author depends on others to reach as many readers' as possible and collect revenues, so it is important for authors to understand how rights – which may include print, digital, audio, visual, dramatization and other formats – are traded and licensed. Authors need to give careful consideration to how, and to whom, they sell various rights in their work.*
>
> – 'How Authors Sell Publishing Rights'
> Helen Sendwick & Orna Ross

When an author sells publishing rights, you are trading a 'license' and this means 'permission to use' and does not mean a transfer of ownership. The writer retains ownership of the copyright, except in limited circumstances such as ghost writing.

Licenses come in many guises from exclusive to non-exclusive. They may be limited to a particular use (educational, non-commercial), or format (print, ebook, audio), or duration or territory.

The purpose of selling rights is to expand a book's readership, and in most cases make a profit or at the very least cover production costs.

Whether you are using a traditional publisher or self-publishing, the act of publishing is always a collaboration. You need editors and a designer to create a good book and you need distributors, retailers and marketing to publish effectively and get maximum leverage from your book.

Traditionally 'rights' have been divided into:

- Volume Rights: the first right to publish the book in the author's language, in volume form.
- Subsidiary Rights: the right to publish the book, or parts of it, in other languages or formats or parts.

For examples of Subsidiary Rights see the Glossary.

As a self-publishing author, your primary contract will be with your self-publishing service provider, or most likely a variety of online retailers like Amazon, Apple iBooks, Kobo, or IngramSpark. For the majority of authors, the primary rights include ebooks, POD and audio.

For more details on how online distributors deliver their contracts, see chapter 16.

TERRITORY

The English language publishing world is traditionally divided across two markets – the US and the UK, which includes Commonwealth countries. When the sale of books was strictly through bookstores, publishers could control these territories; however, now with online selling of books, this has been made more difficult.

If negotiating with a traditional publisher, do not be surprised to find that they will begin by asking for a wide-ranging licence, including all territories and subsidiary rights to all formats of your book. This increases the chance of the publisher making money from the deal and can make it a commercially viable option for them.

The publisher will be counting on overseas deals, book club deals, serial rights, and foreign language packages to help ensure your book is profitable.

The upshot of this chapter primarily is – it is in your best interests to understand the basics of any contract you are signing, whether that is in person or with an online distributor. Understand your rights and exactly what it is you are signing. If you have any doubts seek legal advice. Remember the old saying, 'If it seems too good to be true, it probably is'.

What has been covered here is a very brief overview of what can be a complex system, but if you are working with a trusted self-publishing service provider or a team of editors and designers, you should be retaining all your rights. If you are being signed with a traditional publisher, understand your license agreement and to what formats and territories you are granting them the license.

This is one area of publishing we have all heard horror stories about, but if you keep a level head and don't sign anything under pressure you should be able to avoid the sharks. If someone says, 'This contract has to be signed today or the contract won't go through' – run!

TOP *tips*

1. Understand any contract you are signing.

2. Seek legal advice where necessary.

3. Seek permission to quote or reproduce content.

4. Understand publishing rights.

5. Don't sign away subsidiary rights unless the publisher plans to use them.

CHAPTER 14
Metadata explained and why it is too important to ignore

Metadata is data about data, and in the ebook world metadata is data that describes your book. Understanding and making good use of metadata makes your book more discoverable and accessible to readers.

Your book title is metadata. As is your book description, price, genre, virtually any piece of information that describes and identifies your book is metadata. The possibilities for metadata are virtually unlimited and we will see new types of metadata in the years ahead.

This chapter takes a brief look at what aspects of your book comprises metadata and what you can do to ensure you benefit from addressing every detail.

BOOK TITLE

Your book title is one of the most important pieces of metadata. A good book title grabs the reader and reinforces the message portrayed by the cover image. This includes your subtitle, which should inform the reader the exact subject of your book.

AUTHOR NAME

Your author name is your brand, and for most authors it is their real name. Avoid cutesy spelling as this can make it difficult for readers to find you. Anything that makes it more difficult to find you makes your book less visible. Avoid initials. If your pen name is A.M. Wilson and someone goes to a retailer, either online or a physical bookstore, and searches for AM Wilson (no full stops or spaces) or any combination, the result may come up empty.

BOOK DESCRIPTION/BLURB

This is a short promotional description that appears on the back cover or inside of a book. This is one of the most important pieces of writing you will do for your book.

For ebooks, the book description is equivalent to the jacket copy of a printed book. A good book description is tailored to your target audience and tells the reader something about your writing talent or lack thereof. Do not upload your book with a description that has spelling errors, missing punctuation or grammatical errors. Nothing screams, 'Don't read this book!' faster than typos.

An optimal book description will be clear, compelling and clever.

In a few seconds, readers need to get the gist of your book.

It needs to compel people to read it, which can be achieved by explaining how your book adds value to their life.

Use the common keywords for your genre. This will aid discoverability when people search.

CATEGORY

Another important piece of metadata to consider is the book categories that you list. Think of a category as the online equivalent of the sections and shelves in a traditional bookstore. To maximise your exposure to potential readers, cross-categorise by picking two different categories and subcategories. For example: 'Self Help' and 'Business & Money'.

KEYWORDS

Keywords refer to the words people type into a search engine to locate something. Ideally keywords are words that potential readers will use for conducting searches.

For example: if someone is planning to start their own online business, they might search for, 'How to start an online business'. Optimising the title or subtitle with relevant keywords, for example: '101 Tips to Starting an Online Business', aids the search engine in ensuring your book is visible. Titles and subtitles can be optimised to aid visibility, but only do this if it produces a powerful title. Don't overdo it.

AUTO-GENERATED METADATA

This is automatically produced data and can include your ebook sample and your sales rank within each online reseller.

COVER IMAGE

The cover image is also considered a form of metadata as it helps describe your book.

Even if you are only considering printing your book and giving it away, metadata is still an important aspect to consider. Great metadata will help in making you more visible to your potential readers and customers, and who knows what the future holds in terms of distribution and your book's success.

The following is an example from Amazon about what *not* to do, see if you can spot the typos.

Publishing and Printing Terminology for Self-Publishers: A Seriously Useful Author's Guide Paperback – November 30, 2009

by Jane Rowland ▾ (Author)

Be the first to review this item

› See all formats and editions

**Paperback
from $18.76**

2 Used from $22.29
5 New from $18.76

The publishing world has its own set of words, phrases and standards that can sometimes seem bewildering for a self publishing author. This consise guide is a amzingly useful glossary of all the words and phrases you will encounter when dealing with printers, the books trade, publishers and self publishing services providers. As well as helping guide you through the words and phrases you'll find in standard use within the publishing world, It is also crammed full of insider information which will help you to fet the very best out of your elf publishing experience. Self-publishing has never been as popular as it is today. This guide, written by the Editor of The Self-Publishing magazine, is essential reading if you are planning to self-publish a book.

This is not an example of metadata being used wisely. I do not read this and think 'professional'. I read this and think 'dodgy'. And yes, we all make mistakes and typos. I know I do, especially if I am rushing. The key is not to ignore it but update and correct errors. So, if you do happen to notice a typo in your text, log into your account and update the blurb, don't leave it there.

Metadata is the online tool to ensure you are discovered and can be used freely to your advantage.

TOP
tips

1. All data is metadata.

2. Research categories and keywords.

3. Use online tools to research what keywords people are searching for.

4. Proofread your metadata.

{

CHAPTER 15

Print, ebook or both

Self-publishing a business book will generally mean you wish to publish a book that presents value – it's essentially a business card on steroids – and that can only be achieved with a printed book. While an ebook is important to have for visibility and reach, it does not have the same 'thud' value as a printed book.

Changes in printing technology have been a game changer for self-published authors. Not so many years ago it was easy to pick a book that was 'self-published'. Not only were they often poorly designed, but the printing was poor quality. The paper was cheap and the binding was loose and the laminate on the cover would peel off easily. Self-publishers would often print lower quantities and this low standard was all that was available, and it was expensive. This has all changed now.

The best cover and beautifully formatted book will mean nothing if you do not produce a high-quality printed book. A poorly printed book on cheap paper that does not feel nice to touch will not be read and will be a poor reflection on you and your business.

This chapter examines the different printing options and what to look out for, and the differences in digital files.

PRINTING OPTIONS

Whether you are managing the printing yourself or your self-publishing company is handling this for you, it is helpful to understand the different printing methods and what is involved in the process.

OFFSET PRINTING

Offset printing is printing on a large scale. Everything about it is large and done on an industrial scale. Offset printing is only economical for larger print runs, generally somewhere around a thousand and above. For most self-published authors this will not be a viable option.

DIGITAL PRINTING

Publishing has been transformed by the digital revolution and printing has been one of the major beneficiaries of this. Unlike offset printing presses, a digital printer is not a large industrial sized machine.

Digital printing has been around for years, but it has only been in the last few years that the quality has improved to the point where it can be hard to pick an offset and digitally printed book. One of the biggest improvements with digital printing is the binding of the book. In the past, books could be bound tightly, making them hard to read, or they were loose and fell apart easily.

The advancements in technologies and the growth of self-publishing short-run printing have meant prices have come down dramatically. It's possible to print 100 or so copies of your book that you are proud of, no longer looking like the poor cousin to the 'traditionally published' book.

PRINT ON DEMAND (POD)

POD is at the extreme end of digital printing. It allows you to have a single copy of your book printed to a quality you will be happy with.

Through companies such as Lightning Source, which has plants and offices worldwide with one in Melbourne, you can have your book available in bookshops (if you use a distributor) and to order on sites, such as Amazon (CreateSpace), without printing a single copy in advance.

It is only after your book has been ordered by a bookstore or on a website that the book is printed. The printer prints, binds and mails out your book within days of the order and the reader never knows that it was only printed when they ordered it.

If you set up an account with a POD you can print as many copies as you like, one, ten, a hundred. You can order books yourself and have them delivered directly to your door or shipped directly to your client. Small publishers often use this method for their printing and distribution.

WHICH METHOD IS BEST FOR YOU?

The method you choose to print your book will largely depend on your goals and requirements, and it might change from time to time.

If you plan to do a small print run of a few hundred books, then a digital print run would suit you. If you are planning a print run over 2000 copies, it would best be done using offset printing. However, if you are planning a run of around a thousand books, it is best to get quotes for both offset and digital. Some printers do both and can tell you the difference in cost. You may well want to test the waters and only use print on demand printing a few copies at a time.

For the vast number of self-publishers, the quality of digital printing is fine. However, if the success of your book largely depends on the print quality, such as a full-colour design book or cookbook, then offset printing will give you a far superior finish. The image resolution is a little better as is the quality of the colour and higher quality paper is usually available. The costs will be higher but if you are producing a high-end book, offset printing will give you the results you desire.

CHOOSING A PRINTER

The two major printers we send work to in Australia are Griffin Press and McPherson's Printing. These are used by Australia's major publishers but also work with self-publishers. There are also many smaller printers and general print shops who offer book printing.

The best thing to do is call a couple of printers and discuss your book project to see if they can help. The three things you need to discuss are cost, quality and timeframes. If you are using a smaller printer ask to see a copy of a book they have recently printed, and make sure you specify you want to see a book not a brochure.

If they are not happy to do this, perhaps you should look elsewhere. Printing is like designing a book cover, not all graphic designers can design a cover, not all printers print quality books. Some say they can but have no real interest in producing a quality book.

Now is not the time to drop the bundle. Even though it may have taken you a long time to get to this point, and you just want the book printed and done, try not to rush through this stage of self-publishing. Believe me, there is nothing worse than waiting with anticipation for your book to arrive, opening the box, and having your heart sink because the book is not at all what you imagined and you are back to square one, ultimately, having wasted your time and money.

Things to look out for in sample copy:

- Is the paper good quality?
- Does the book feel high quality or does it feel cheap?
- Do the images appear sharp and clear?
- Is the cover aligned?

- Is the printing tone even?
- Is the binding solid and easy to open?

If you are happy with the quality, now is the time to get a quote. For them to supply you with an accurate quote you will need to supply them with the following information:

- How many copies you want printed. Get quotes for a couple of different size print runs.
- Your book size, commonly known in publishing as the 'trim size'.
- The page extent of your book, don't forget the prelims and endmatter.
- Does it have any colour internally?
- Delivery site – Australia or International.
- Type of binding.
- Type of lamination.
- Type of paper for text and cover.

Don't hesitate to ask questions of either your self-publishing company or your printer. Both should be more than happy to spend time with you to help you understand the process involved. If not, it might be time to get further quotes and samples.

For more details on printing specifications and paper stock see the Glossary.

THE EBOOK

As we are all aware industries working in digital technology have had a huge shake up in the past decade. The way we take and store photos, listen to music, watch television, videos and movies, and the way we read books have all been transformed.

Who knows what we will be doing in the next decade; however, one thing is for sure, this is a constantly changing landscape and things will continue to evolve. Any businesses who do not change and adapt will quickly be redundant and fail to survive. You only have to look at Kodak and Video Easy to see examples of businesses not moving with the times.

Digital technology has seen the rise of the ebook and they have some huge advantages. A reader can download a book at anytime from anywhere they have internet access and read your book from a digital device. They are also comparatively cheaper than a printed book. On the downside they can be limited in how they can be formatted and they do not have the 'thud' value of a printed book.

EBOOK FORMATS

There are a number of different options to consider before converting your book to an ebook for use on tablets, smartphones and e-reader devices. The most common is epub and you will need a mobi file for Amazon.

EPUB

Epub is the most widely used ebook format and stands for 'electronic publication'. It displays on most smartphones/tablets (with the exception of Amazon Kindle e-reader).

Epub comes in 2 styles: reflowable epub and fixed-layout epub. Reflowable epub means the text will flow dynamically to fill the length of your device, wrap to the edges of the screen, and it allows user control to increase/decrease font size for readability. It also features searchable text and supports colour images/text. This type of epub is used mainly for novels and nonfiction books, which are text heavy. The downside of reflowable text is that your ebook is limited in its formatting and will not appear the same as your printed book.

Fixed-layout epubs appear exactly as the printed version. On most devices, fixed-layout epubs will open up as double-page spreads, just like reading a book. Text, images and other page elements are in fixed positions on the page – there is no option for users to increase/ decrease font size to enhance readability. This type of epub is used mainly for cookbooks, picture books and other books with many in-text images.

Epub files can have a few glitches and you may experience minor errors in the layout such as inconsistent text sizes or lists and tables not lining up. If your book is heavily styled with diagrams, charts and images, you may well feel a little uninspired by the epub file, especially compared with your printed book.

EPDF

Epdf is an ebook format converted from a PDF, with 'Table of Contents' support on ebook-reading software. Appearance-wise, it will look exactly as the printed version, like a fixed-layout epub. However, unlike a fixed-layout epub, epdfs do not display as double-page spreads – but one page at a time. It doesn't allow increasing/ decreasing the size of fonts. Epdfs are suitable for reading on any smartphone or tablet, but not Amazon Kindle. Epdfs are not supported for sale on Apple iBooks Store, or Amazon EBook store.

WHY USE AN EPDF?

The main advantage of an epdf over other ebook formats is its ability to preserve the original layout of any document – text, illustrations, photos, maps – a 'what you see is what you get' format. The compatibility of epdf with all computers, smartphone and tablet devices, gives readers more flexibility on how they view your ebook.

MOBI

Mobi is an ebook format for exclusive use on the Amazon Kindle and sale on the Amazon ebook store. It is not supported by Apple iPhones, iPads and Android devices. This format is very limited and bare bones in its appearance. Most versions of the Kindle do not support colour display. Most ebook conversion services will supply you with an epub file and a mobi file.

EBOOK PRICING

Ebook pricing is a tricky thing and will largely depend on your goals and requirements. If you would like to gain traction early in your book launch, you can release your book for free or 99 cents for a limited time. With the right promotion this can help you get the sought after 'Bestselling Author Badge'. The key to remember with online distribution is you can adjust your price to see how this reflects sales and profits – just don't do it too often or you will potentially annoy your readers.

As with any publishing decision, do your research. Look at other books in your categories and see what they are selling for. If the majority of books are $2.99, this might be an indication that this is all the market is willing to pay. This does not mean this is what your book is worth, of course it is worth much more, but it is what readers are willing to pay.

Amazon and various other companies are consistently conducting research and $10 seems to be the price point where ebook sales significantly drop off. With this in mind, I would only suggest pricing your ebook over $10 if it is highly specialised or for the high-end market.

For the majority of self-publishing entrepreneurs, profit from book sales is not the primary goal, visibility and credibility is. It is up to you to weigh up what is important to you, profit on each book sale or more sales.

DIGITAL RIGHTS MANAGEMENT

Digital Rights Management or DRM may not be a term you are familiar with but you will be aware of the concept. Ebooks, like music and any other digital products, can be easily copied and distributed illegally. In essence DRM is copyright management placed on the files when they are sold. The files are encoded so that the person buying them can be the only person allowed to use the file, so the file can't be copied. Has this technology worked for publishers? It seems not. Computer hackers are smart, and as fast as publishers update technology, hackers work out a way around it.

The downside of DRM for readers is that it locks them into a single device and platform. Some argue that DRM actually encourages piracy as readers want to use their ebooks how they like. And if you think of a printed book, once you buy it you can share it with as many people as you like. It is not a 'one read only' book.

Do you apply DRM or not? In some instances you won't have a choice, the online retailer will automatically apply DRM. At other times you can choose. Most authors still choose to have DRM but we generally don't recommend it. Times have changed and there really is no way to protect your data – if someone wants to hack your file they probably will. And the more people who read your book the greater your visibility, even if they didn't pay for the pleasure, they still know you.

Deciding to have a printed book, ebook or both is an important decision and we always suggest people chose both. This gives readers the flexibility of an ebook, and it gives you a powerful leveraging tool and instant credibility. Nothing says published author like a printed book, and it's a constant reminder of you and your business.

TOP *tips*

1. Research printers.

2. Choose the type of printing you will use.

3. Obtain several quotes for various print runs.

4. Decide on print specifications, including paper stock, cover laminate etc.

5. Have your files converted to epub and mobi.

CHAPTER 16
Distribution channels – which is the best option for you?

Deciding how to distribute your book can be as confusing as any other stage of the publishing journey. As the author of a nonfiction business book, how you distribute your book can influence its power as a leveraging tool.

This chapter looks at the various ways you can distribute your book both physically and online.

BOOKSTORES

Getting a self-published book into bookstores is difficult, not impossible, but difficult. One key element is to produce a professional book that the reader would think is a traditionally published book. You can approach this one of two ways – doing it yourself or using a book distributor.

DIY BOOKSTORE DISTRIBUTION

It is understandable that most bookstores are reluctant to take on a self-published author who probably only has one book for sale and little to no sales history. They have to set up an account, order separately, define your terms of trade, and they have no guarantee that your book will sell more than one or two copies.

The main advantage to not using a distributor is the cost saving. Usually a distributor will take 60 to 70 per cent of the RRP. They keep 15 to 20 per cent as their fee and pass the remainder onto the bookstore. Thereby you save the 15 to 20 per cent but you need to calculate if this saving is worth the time and energy involved. Selling your book for a profit is not where the benefits lie, being visible is where leveraging comes into its own.

If you do decide it is worth the effort, the first thing you need to do is make contact with the bookstores. You can send out sample copies of your book and include your contact details and any information about how to order. Visit your local bookstores and introduce yourself, especially smaller independent bookstores. Don't take it personally if they say, 'Thanks but no thanks, we don't deal with self-publishers'.

You can announce your book in various industry publications such as the magazine *Books & Publishing*, which is widely read in the publishing industry. Generating publicity around your book is a useful way of getting into bookstores. If you can gain some media interest, bookstores may well contact you to stock your book.

The downside of going down the DIY route is both the time it takes to get into a bookstore and the time it takes to manage the distribution, especially if your book is successful. The last thing you want is to be spending hours packaging up the books, posting them out and managing the account.

BOOKSTORE DISTRIBUTION COMPANIES

There are a number of excellent book distributors in Australia, both large and small, who will get your book into bookstores. There is an application process and not all books are accepted, but producing a professional book helps this process.

What you get for the 15 to 20 per cent fee is that they take all the stress out of bookstore distribution. They deal with the stores, invoicing and sending out the book. In the eyes of a bookstore, your book is at its peak potential when it is new and has media interest. If you decide to go the DIY route first to see if it works, you potentially lose this opportunity.

ONLINE DISTRIBUTION

The advent of global online distribution has been one of the great levellers in publishing, making it possible to have your book available as an ebook or print on demand to anyone globally. Five companies are currently at the forefront of the self-publishing space, in terms of quality of service, ability to reach readers, and fairness of terms.

Other than Amazon's KDP Select, all deliver non-exclusive contracts and allow authors to keep all publishing rights. They base their business model on sales commission not rights licensing.

1. **Amazon** – has the lion's share of market dominance and is generally an independent author's first port of call. Amazon is constantly adding new features, changing its terms and conditions and how it operates. Please check directly on Amazon's advice pages and on kindle boards (forums) for the latest up-to-date terms. Kindle is the online ebook reseller and CreateSpace is the print on demand reseller.

2. **Apple iBooks** – is available for all iOS capable products, allowing readers to take their library with them on the go. This enables the reader to sync devices – laptop, ipad, iphone – and allows them to switch between devices. You must own a Mac to create a book on iBook. There are restrictions around mentioning third party book retailers, which can make iBooks more of a hassle than Kindle to set up, but terms and conditions are generally better than Amazon.

3. **IngramSpark** – is unique in that it offers ebook and print distribution through the same platform. You can use it for one or the other, or both.

4. **Kobo** – features an open platform that supports multiple digital formats in over 100 languages in 190 countries. The upload is simple and highly user friendly, and authors can modify how they control their rights.

5. **Nook** – this is the the name of the Barnes & Noble tablets and eReader applications. Nook offers an application for Mac, Windows, iOS, Android, and online reading. To get started you use a service called Nook Press. Nook Press allows authors to upload a Word document; however, to achieve the most accurate conversion of your manuscript to a book on Nook readers, you are advised to upload an epub file.

EBOOK UPLOADING

Most ebook stores allow you to upload your ebook yourself. If you are reasonably computer savvy you should have no trouble setting up your account and uploading your files. It can be time-consuming and hiccups can occur along the way, so I suggest you don't leave it until the night before your launch to get started. Different sites will require different information, and once again you need to decide if the saving made by doing it yourself is worth the time it takes.

Your self-publishing service provider may offer this service as part of your package or you could use aggregator sites such as Smashwords. Smashwords is an ebook distributor working on a 15 per cent commission. It does not offer design and editing services. Smashwords focuses on ebook resellers, such as Apple, Barnes & Noble, Kobo and Sony – but not Amazon. Readers can also buy directly from its website.

DIGITAL DIRECT SALES

You can sell your ebooks via Gumroad, E-Junkie, Clickbank and a host of other companies. Your files are placed on the service and a link is added to your website. People can click on the link, pay for the file and download it. The author pays a transaction and a hosting fee. You can also sell your book directly from your own website or social media.

AUDIO BOOKS

Audio is booming and is an area that is expanding the opportunities for indie authors.

Humans have been listening to stories for millennia. Look at how Indigenous Australians have kept their history and culture alive through telling the stories of Dreamtime. People can multitask while listening to an audio book, which allows them to read on the go. Before signing any contracts check to see who holds the right to audio.

THINGS TO CONSIDER

Below is a list of aspects to keep in mind when considering your distribution channel.

Royalties

This is the payment made to you, the author, from the distributor, or in the case of traditional publishing, from the publisher. The rates vary depending on where you choose to distribute your book. For the best royalty rates go directly to the individual retailer. Each site has detailed help and you don't need any programming skills to use them.

Global Territories

When selling through Amazon you can reach multiple territories. These are accessed through your account. Click on your book cover and edit it if necessary. Save and go to the second page. This is the 'Rights and Pricing' page. It is here that you assign rights to sell your book in different countries. These need to be considered when choosing KDP royalty deals. It is important to regularly check your account as territories can be updated and expanded.

Foreign Rights

Having your book on as many online distributers' sites as possible worldwide, allows for a greater readership reach. If by chance an editor or someone in a translation house sees your book and is interested, they may contact you directly offering you a foreign rights contract. Or if you are not happy to leave this to chance your best option is to hire a literary agent. Do your research when hiring a foreign rights agency, find one who is established and has a good reputation among the publishers.

Pricing and Distribution

A publisher sets a book's recommended retail price (RRP) and then generally this is how the distribution chain works:

- Publisher sells book to distributor or wholesaler with up to 70 per cent discount on RRP.
- Distributor or wholesaler sells to book retailer at 40 to 55 per cent discount.
- Retailer sells at whatever price.
- Books that don't sell are returned.

Publisher RRP $15
Distributor Buys @ $4.50
Distributor Sells @ $7.50
Retailer Sells @ $12.99

Categories and Keywords

When setting up your online distribution accounts you will need to choose categories to be listed under. As mentioned previously, think of a category as the section of the bookshop where your book would be placed. Amazon has thousands of categories to choose from and books have been written about how to choose the best one.

Spend some time learning how 'Amazon sales ranks' work, and research the bestselling books in the categories you are considering. This will give you an indication as to how many books you need to sell to become a bestselling author. Sales ranks are adjusted constantly and are based on your recent sales and are separate for paid and free book sales. Your book can only be ranked for one at a time.

For more information on choosing a category visit my website www.independentink.com.au and download the free guide.

Amazon and Author Central

An important step in creating a visible profile on Amazon is located in the Author Central section of your account. Creating this will set you apart from the vast number of authors selling their books on Amazon.

After you create your Amazon account at kdp.amazon.com and your book is uploaded, you will be able to create your Author Central account. For the best results, add a picture, bio and all other available options. Ensure that you include a link to your book, including the book description.

The more widely available your book is for sale, the greater opportunity your reader has for purchasing your book.

Start considering all of these options well before your book launch to ensure everything goes according to plan.

TOP
tips

1. Research book distributors to bookstores.

2. Choose online distributors for both print and ebook.

3. Set up accounts a week before launch date.

4. Spend time researching which categories to be listed under.

5. Don't forget to upload your author bio.

SECTION THREE

{ Building your author platform }

{

CHAPTER 17

What is an author platform?

The good and the bad news about being a published author is that it is up to you to promote and market your book. This is the case whether you are using a traditional publisher or self-publishing.

In the majority of cases a traditional publisher will not even consider an emerging author unless they can clearly prove that they have established an impressive author platform. This is an indication of the importance that the publishing industry as a whole places on a great author platform.

But what is an author platform? This chapter looks at the author platform on a general level. Again, a complete book could be written about how you develop a platform, and fundamentally this is the same whether you are an author, preparing to become an influential leader, or desire a presence in your field. Everyone has a different definition on how this can be achieved. For some the image of standing on a stage staring out to an audience comes to mind, sending chills down their spine. For others the shear idea of self-promotion makes them go weak at the knees, only to shove this important step to the bottom of the to-do list.

WHAT IT ISN'T

So firstly, let's take the fear out of 'Building a Platform', and clearly define what it is *not*:

- It is not about selling.
- It is not about 'Look at me, Kymmie'.
- It is not about annoying people.
- It is not about being a show pony.
- It is not something you can buy.
- It is not something that will happen overnight.

WHAT IT IS ABOUT?

Having a clear understanding about what an author platform is, helps in taking the mystery out of it. If you are currently in business you will most likely have a number of these things already in place. As an entrepreneur you will be relatively comfortable promoting your business, and building an author platform is very similar but the focus is now on you, the business owner.

Some argue that if a business currently doesn't have a website and an online presence they will be out of business in five years. This is subjective but should be a wakeup call for anyone in business who is still struggling to come to terms with the changes in digital technology and what this has meant for both business and publishing.

Without having a presence both online and in the real world it is near impossible to establish a successful platform.

FOUR KEY AREAS TO CONSIDER

There are four key areas to consider when deciding how to develop your author platform.

Visibility

Who knows you, who is aware of the work you do, where is your work published and seen, what communities are you involved with and are you active in these communities, who do you influence? The important point to remember here is to focus on your target market. There is very little value in building your author profile with a market that has no interest, or need in what value you can give them.

Some of the areas to think about are:

- Do you write articles that have been published?
- Are you a regular guest speaker?
- Do you attend networking events?
- Are you called upon by the media to make comments on events in your field?
- Do you write blog posts?
- Are you active on social media?

These are only some of the ways to become visible with your target market and this is covered in more detail in the following chapters.

Authority

What is your credibility? This is particularly important for nonfiction writers, as your readers will be looking for this credibility in one form or another. In this age of 24-hour media, we have become very time poor and very wary, and we will only devote our time and energy on something or someone who has perceived authority.

Some of the areas to think about:

- How long have you been in business?
- Do you hold any industry awards?
- Who are your trusted clients?

- Do you have any partnerships?
- Do you hold industry qualifications?
- Do you have testimonials from influential people?
- Do you have proven statistics?

Depending on the industry you are in, the method of establishing your authority will vary. The key point to remember here is that writing a great book is one way that will most definitely help to build your authority and credibility.

Proven Reach

It is not enough to say you have visibility, you need to be able to prove it and the impact that you have. As a self-published author, proving your reach is a valuable exercise to give you a clear indication on what is working and what needs improvement.

If you are looking to pitch to a traditional publisher, this will be a very important part of proving your book has merit and has an already established network to promote to. Publishers' marketing budgets are limited, especially for new authors, and a proven reach will give the publisher an indication that you are established and less of a risk.

Some areas to look at are:

- The size of your email list.
- Do you regularly contact your email list with great content?
- Does your list engage with this content?
- Does your website get a lot of traffic?
- Do your blog posts get regularly reviewed and commented on?
- Do you have an active social media following? Are people 'liking' and 'commenting' on your Twitter, Facebook and LinkedIn posts?

- Do you have reviews and testimonials on your social media and web page? A combination of both works well.

Once again, this is only meant to be a starting point to get you thinking, there are many other ways to prove your reach.

Target Audience

If you have read the beginning chapters of the book you should have a clearer definition of who your target audience is. Everything you do with regard to building your profile should be aimed at the audience you are trying to influence and reach – your niche. The clearer you are on who this is the easier it will be to make a plan on how you are going to achieve your desired results.

THE BENEFITS TO BUILDING AN AUTHOR PLATFORM – THE WHY

Building a platform is about attracting likeminded people who are interested in what problems you can solve. This is best achieved by putting in consistent and focused effort. It can be a lot like the processes involved in writing. It requires scheduling time to prepare articles to publish and needs to be given priority.

How best to build a platform largely depends on where your target market is and who they are. What follows is a list of ideas, but in this constantly changing digital world this is by no means an exhaustive list.

- Publish work/articles in outlets where you want to be recognised and identified as the expert in your field.
- Produce a body of work for your own platform.
- Speaking opportunities.
- Partnering with peers and influencers.
- Social media engagement.

- Build a relationship with the media.
- Sign up to become a source for the media, SourceBottle, which sends out daily emails to their subscribers with call outs and is free.

Some people find building a platform easier than others. Some will already be well known in their industry and be seen as a 'thought leader'. Some may know key people in their industry and can call on this connection to establish introductions. While others may be uncomfortable with the idea of building a platform or are new to their industry, and writing a book is their way of enhancing their credibility.

Platform building is an organic process and there is not a 'one size fits all' solution. A lot will depend on your message, your unique story, your target readership, but most importantly you and your unique strengths and qualities.

WHEN TO START

As an entrepreneur and business owner it is likely that you have already begun building your platform and profile. Creating buzz around your book should begin as soon as you make the commitment to write, the earlier the better.

Letting your audience know in advance that you are in the writing process has the added bonus of motivating you to finish and publish. Do you want to be known as the person who is still writing their book, years after you committed to writing?

The next three chapters are an overview of some of the options available to either begin building your author platform or enhance what you have already created. Like anything it can be hard to get started, and you may feel uncomfortable and out of your comfort zone, but with practice it will get easier and the benefits will far outweigh any pain.

TOP
tips

1. Have a clear understanding of what an author platform is NOT.

2. An author platform is needed for traditional publishing and self-publishing.

3. Write a mind map of where your visibility currently is and how you can expand it. Think about your network.

4. Write a mind map on your authority and credibility.

5. Write a mind map on how you currently reach your market and what can be improved on.

6. Most importantly, building a platform is not about selling or shouting your name to the rooftops. You have a unique perspective on the world and your industry and you have a story to tell. An author platform will help you do this.

CHAPTER 18
Owned platforms: websites, email lists, blogs and more

Marketing is one of those areas that sends shivers down the spines of most authors and entrepreneurs alike. It is common knowledge in the publishing industry, both traditional and indie, that it is with the marketing and promotion that the hard work begins.

As you begin the writing process you should be making plans on how you are going to be promoting your book. Ideally, marketing plans should begin even before pen hits paper.

This chapter looks at building your author platform through marketing channels that you own. The benefit of focusing on platforms that you own is you remain in control. Social media platforms can change their rules and campaigns can be disrupted. You can be deemed to have broken the rules and your social media page can be taken down, often losing all your followers.

Included in this chapter are various social media platforms. Some would argue that you do not own these, you only rent the space. Violate the rules and you can be kicked out. But for ease I have included them here as they are free to set up and you have control over the content uploaded.

THE IMPORTANCE OF PLANNING

Understanding every aspect of marketing channels is near on impossible, as at the time of writing there were over 65 different marketing channels. No one can be a master of all of these. The key is to pick a couple of different platforms to begin with and master these before adding another one or two, if necessary.

When you are planning your 'Digital Marketing Strategy' clearly define what your objectives are and who your target audience is. Working out where your people are takes research, but if you have mind mapped your target market in Chapter 1, you will have a good base on where to start.

Determining your niche and where your tribe is hanging out, will determine what works best for you. There is little point targeting the over 60s on Snapchat and Instagram, as it is unlikely that they are using these platforms. No matter what the statistics say about overall numbers, you need to niche it down. The same goes for targeting tweens, you won't be very successful if you concentrate your marketing efforts and budget on LinkedIn as your preferred platform.

A great place to start in your planning phase is to research your competitors, sign up for their 'opt ins', and see what is and isn't working in your industry. When I was developing my marketing strategy I researched as many local and overseas competitors as I could. I was not only looking at their pricing strategies, but also what opt ins they had.

WEBSITES

As an entrepreneur who is planning to write a book, it is a good bet to presume you already have a website, and if not, why not? If you don't have a website for your business it will be a good idea to set up a personal page to promote you and your book. Andrew Griffiths suggests it is a good idea to have a personal website, but this will depend on your personal preferences, time and budget.

During the writing phase is a good time to start reviewing your website. You don't want to get to the book launch stage and suddenly realise your website is out of date and unprofessional or no longer represents you and your brand. As with most things, website design goes through trends and it is important to be seen as professional.

Things to look out for when reviewing or designing your site are:

- Well-written 'About' page.
- Contact details are visible.
- Clear call to action.
- Easy to navigate.
- Easy type to read.
- Sends the right message.

For most people, talk of 'optimisation' and 'SEO' is like talking in a foreign language. Unless this is of interest to you or your area of expertise, I suggest working with professionals, both web designers and SEO experts, to ensure your site is up to speed.

LEAD GENERATION

Creating lead magnets and building your database prior to your book launch is a valuable asset. This then enables you to contact your database to share details about your book and where they can buy it.

The buzzwords in marketing are all about 'lead generation' and 'lead magnets'.

To capture a prospect's details, you will need to create something of value that they will happily exchange their contact information for. This is called a lead magnet. These can be available as links from your website, social media pages or as part of an email campaign or newsletter. Usually this is in the form of asking your potential prospect to 'opt in' to your list to receive your lead magnet.

There are literally dozens of types of lead magnets, and what works for you will depend on your industry and your target audience. What follows is a brief outline of popular and effective choices.

Ebook

This is one of the most popular and well-known lead magnets. The length and style of your ebook can vary depending on the topic and your target market. They are generally made available as a downloadable PDF after the prospect enters their name and email address in exchange for receiving the ebook.

The common thread among great ebook lead magnets is that they solve a problem for the reader, so it is *not* an opportunity for a hard sell. The key is to keep the solution you are offering simple and easy to achieve. The purpose is to help the reader build a relationship with you.

Some great themes to get you thinking are:

- The 7 Mistakes
- The 3 Steps
- How to guide

Report or Guide

This is very much like the ebook and is typically made available as a PDF download after the user enters their name and email address. The difference with a report or guide is that the reader has an expectation that the information is factual and on a specific issue, timeline or process, whereas an ebook can be more of an opinion piece.

Checklist

A checklist is a great lead magnet as they are relatively easy to produce and have a high-perceived value. Think about what you do in your everyday business, what do you tell your clients now? Checklists can be created to help people keep track of their bills, their exercise schedule, their daily food intake. I have created a checklist around the timeframe of publishing and when you should be doing what, in order to publish on your planned launch date.

Free Trial

Free trials work well if you have a software as a service or other membership services, like a gym or yoga studio. 'Try before you buy' works well as it helps in the beginning to build a relationship and forming trust.

Tool

Creating a tool that will make your prospect's life easier is a powerful lead magnet. Tools vary from simple spreadsheets (social media calendar), a calculator (if you offer financial advice), or even a low-cost physical product.

Free App

This is not the cheapest or easiest option. In most cases this will have to be designed and developed by an outside source, but the benefit is it has a high-perceived value, and if designed well can keep you at the forefront of potential prospects' minds.

Competitions

These are great fun and an easy way to build interest in your product and brand, and they have potential to build your list quickly. You could offer a product, a free consultation, free marketing session, free month's membership. Be creative in deciding what would be of interest to your audience. Your niche will have a certain need that will get them excited and interested enough to sign up to your list.

Infographics

Infographics are a great way to display information in an easy, eye-catching way that readers are more likely to retain. Look on Pinterest for ideas and try sites like DepositPhoto, where you can buy infographics already designed. You then just fill in your information.

USING YOUR LEAD GENERATION TO NURTURE AND GROW YOUR EMAIL LIST

Creating valuable lead magnets and building your database is a wonderful source of owned contacts that you can continue to nurture through email marketing.

We have all heard the experts proclaim that email is dead, but despite this email is still one of the best ways to reach your audience. Your email list is something you own and is a valuable asset that should be regarded highly.

For the statisticians among you, here are a few interesting stats:

- *There are over 4.35 billion email accounts. This figure is predicted to reach 5.59 billion by 2019, which is a growth of more than 26%.* Radicati Group, 2015, www.emailisnotdead.com
- *68% of consumers find email to be their number one preferred channel for receiving commercial messages.* CG Selections Nationaal Email Onderzoek, 2013, www.emailisnotdead.com
- *72% of consumers say that email is their favoured conduit of communication with companies they do business with.* Marketing Sherpa, 2015, www.emailisnotdead.com

Readers/clients who subscribe to your email list do so because they are interested in what you have to share with them. Email is the greatest tool that you own, but owning people's email addresses is a privilege and comes with certain responsibility. It is illegal to spam your list and you must keep information safe.

It is important to keep readers engaged or risk them unsubscribing. One way to do this is to offer free content. This can be in the way of a free chapter or content that solves a problem, as was discussed earlier in lead generation.

Autoresponder

One of the best ways to engage with your readers regularly is to set up an autoresponder. This is a system or software package that is either free or you purchase that manages your email list. Automation is key in increasing the likelihood of a potential customer opening your email, as it has been proven that a greater success rate of opens occurs if the prospect receives your welcome email immediately after they have left their details. This prospect email is incredibly important in your email sequence. It has the highest open rates of all automated emails at 60 to 100 per cent.

The winning formula for a great automated email sequence is firstly to have a plan. Mind map out what your potential customer journey is and what problems you can solve for them. Have your email sequence planned before you launch, with everything designed and ready to go. Follow a theme throughout these emails – it is generally recommended that you have a consistent header and footer with the html code embedded and the central body of text is where you have your message. A great welcome email should be personalised, so it is very important to capture your prospects first name, thank and reward them, and give clear call to actions.

One great advantage of an autoresponder is it allows you to plan and set up your email strategies in advance. In the initial stages of setting up an email list you can work with an excel spreadsheet, but this will quickly become hard to run and you will start running into issues, especially if you are using a gmail or hotmail account.

Using an autoresponder will also have a dramatic increase in the rate of deliverability of your emails, and depending on which one you are using deliverability can be as high as 98 per cent. The last thing you want to happen after spending hours working on your email strategy is finding a large percentage of your emails in the junk/spam box.

They also help ensure that you are following the anti-spam laws by automatically including an unsubscribe button that allows anyone on the list to quickly and easily unsubscribe to your emails.

EBanner

You can manage a series of emails ahead of time, setting the time and date each email is to be sent. You can also alter this depending on how the recipient responds to your previous email. For example: they have requested a download of your ebook to be sent to them but they do not click on the email and open it. You can set up a series of emails to resend the book or perhaps other information relevant to what the reader might be looking for. Your autoresponder immediately responds to your promises, making you appear professional and credible.

You can also send out a newsletter or notification to your list at any time. This can be written in advance and scheduled. Say if you have a book launch coming up, you can write a series of emails notifying your list of the upcoming launch and how they can buy your book, or if you are doing a promotion you can let them be the first to know.

The other thing an autoresponder allows you to do is run split tests. If you are unsure if your subject lines are capturing your reader's attention you can run a split test, sending half your list one subject line and the other half a different one. By studying the analytics you can determine which one has the better open rates.

You can also do a split test for your book title if you are struggling to pick one over another. Half the list receives an email with one title as the subject line and the other half the other title. Studying the analytics of the open rates will give you an indication as to which title your potential readers found more engaging.

As far as data goes it is from the backend of the autoresponder that you will garnish the most insights. By studying the analytics you can determine a vast amount of useful information about your list. For example: it can show you how many people opened your email, email opt ins, unsubscribes etc.

It is important to set aside time on a regular basis to analyse your open rates, click rates, and how your list is performing. Bigger lists are not necessarily better. Small groups of targeted, engaged readers are far more effective and valuable than a large list of unengaged readers who never click on your email and just hit the delete button. Learning how to read the numbers will be a valuable tool in helping you look at and understand what is working and what isn't.

You will spend many hours working on your emails and this can be a waste of valuable time and resources if your emails are not being effective.

Some autoresponders currently on the market:

- MailChimp
- Infusion Soft
- Sales Force

For great tips on how to convert customers into leads using targeted emails, check out the book *Conversion* by Justine Coombe.

THE BUYER'S JOURNEY

You may well be asking, 'Why do all this? How will this help my book and my business?' These are valid questions and can be answered by looking into the buyer's journey.

The way customers are buying has fundamentally changed. Google has done considerable research into this area and have coined the phrase 'Zero Moment of Truth' (ZMOT). ZMOT has been described as a revolution in the way shoppers decide to purchase.

Look at your own shopping habits and how they have changed. Now with Google we can research any product at any time of the day, from the comfort of your living room couch. How often do you grab the iPad during the ad breaks and do some online searching?

The ZMOT is the moment when an individual decides they will in fact purchase the product to fulfil their need. Once this decision has been made they will begin searching for the product or service until they are ready to make their purchase.

Unless you are visible in the market place, your potential prospect doesn't even know you exist. A significant finding from the Google study was that prospects are not ready to buy at the first touch point with the product or service. It was found that this increased as the individual had consumed seven hours of interaction with the brand, its products or services. And this is through eleven points of contact via four different mediums. This is where the use of a variety of different tools comes into its own.

Blog Post

Writing regular blog posts is a great way to share content. This can be a lead into your book, or helpful tips and tools that will help your customers and potential readers.

Writing a blog is where you can share your lead magnet or introduce a link to some free content. For topic ideas, read other people's blogs and ask yourself if there are interesting developments in your industry, and read online news sources such as Inc. and Huffington Post.

Repurpose content from your book into blog posts – this can be outsourced if you are too busy, so look online at sites like Upworks and fiverr. Once written and proofread, these can be uploaded to your website and shared on social media.

Podcasts

Podcasts are a great way to build your profile and interest in your book; either produce your own or be a guest on other podcasts. They are also a great way to build relationships with your audience. How often do you listen to a podcast and feel like you know the speaker, you gain an insight into who they are and their values. A small connection is developed.

Webinars

Offering free or low-cost webinars are a powerful way of building your profile and trust within your community. Do you have something that you do that you could offer online to a wider audience? An accounting business could offer a series of short webinars on how to prepare for end of year, saving clients time and money on having their end of year financials prepared.

Video

Video is the latest tool people are frequently using to share content. This can be embedded on your web page, shared on social media or you can create your own YouTube channel. Video is a great way of allowing people to get to know you and build buyer trust.

Social Media

Recently I was at an event and social media platforms were explained as the following.

Twitter is like standing around the office water cooler, gossiping, conversations come and go and they are not lasting. Facebook is more social and is like sitting around your dining room table. You establish conversations and build relationships in a friendly social manner. LinkedIn is the equivalent of sitting at the board room table with a room full of business executives.

Each has a different tone of conversation, and what is said and shared on Twitter won't necessarily be shared on LinkedIn. Knowing where your tribe is hanging out is paramount in determining where your time and effort is best spent.

Social media is the tool you use to share the content you are posting on your website. It is great that you have developed a wealth of information on your website but it is not going to be discovered unless you promote it. The best part of promoting valuable free information on social media is if someone likes it they will share it with their networks.

Twitter

As a recent convert to Twitter, I am still getting my head around how to tweet and how the Twitter universe works. Even in my relatively short time on Twitter, I have found it easier to engage directly with authors and industry thought leaders on Twitter than I have on other platforms. Valerie Khoo from the Australian Writers Centre finds Twitter the most useful way to share her content.

A word of warning though, Twitter can be addictive and you can find yourself mindlessly 'wasting' hours checking your Twitter feed.

Facebook

If used well Facebook is a powerful tool to reach potential customers and engage with your audience. Facebook's new rules and algorithms have made it more difficult to have the same reach for free as it did in the past, but it is still possible. Blog posts can be shared, customers can be kept updated about new releases, links to sales pages can be shared and you can also share other businesses' information who have a similar target audience. Once again, you are limited only by your imagination and Facebook's rules on what is acceptable.

LinkedIn

LinkedIn is the boardroom of social media and can be a powerful tool in professional networking. Spend time setting up or reviewing your profile. Make sure you have a professional headshot. Don't use your wedding photo, no matter how beautiful you look. LinkedIn is the place you want to be seen as a professional.

Other Platforms

The number of social media platforms is constantly updating and trends come and go and are very dependent on your niche.

Some other popular platforms are:

- Instagram
- Pinterst
- Snapchat

The important thing to remember across all platforms is it is all about the conversation – not the sales spiel:

- Don't just promote yourself.
- Use the 80/20 rule: 80% helpful content, 20% marketing your product.
- Respond to people and engage in conversations.
- Thank people who share your content.
- Connect with influencers in your industry.

TOP
tips

1. Plan your digital marketing strategy, don't leave this to chance.

2. Clearly define your target audience.

3. Research where they hang out.

4. Update your website.

5. Create lead magnets that work for your tribe.

6. Don't underestimate the value of your email list.

7. Connect with your audience and build relationships.

{
Paid: advertising for social media, google ad words and more

Your book is a great way to build publicity, and one way to help do this is through paid advertising. But before you book the half page ad in your chosen publication, think about how you could get an article written about you and your book in that same publication. Thereby, giving you greater exposure for free. Advertising, like many other industries has changed and it is important to understand the dynamics of the playing field to ensure you not only get value for money but results.

This chapter looks at the changing landscape of paid advertising and how you can use cost-effective strategies to maximum effect. The days of running full-page ads in newspapers and magazines are dying and can be seen in the demise of many traditional publications. Much like publishing, the world of advertising has been turned on its head with the rise of social media and online publications.

PAID ONLINE ADVERTISING

Before commencing any paid online advertising campaign ensure that you have your Google page setup. This means that when someone Googles you your details appear on the right-hand side of the screen. Asking customers to add a review enhances your presence and credibility.

Examples of paid online advertising include Google Adwords, Facebook promotions, LinkedIn and paid Twitter promotions. With all platforms you can set up daily spends, select target audiences and total budget. In the backend of the sites you can analyse the data and reach of your ad, and look to see if it has been effective. Never before have such comprehensive data analysis tools been available.

This type of advertising is a good, cheap way to conduct split testing to work out what works in getting engagement and clicks.

RETARGETING

Retargeting is all about building your presence with people who have already been on your website. If someone visits your web page and you have the Facebook pixel installed, you can set up an ad to retarget them in their Facebook feed. Do you ever notice how after you have been on a site for cat food, Facebook magically knows you are looking at cat food and a sponsored post appears? This is not magic – it is retargeting and can be very effective in building brand awareness both for your business and your book.

PAID INFLUENCERS

We have all seen paid influencers in traditional advertising. Sportsmen and actors will often be seen as the face of a particular product. They are paid to promote the product or service on an ongoing basis, not a one-off advertisement. This will be outside the realms of most of our initial budgets, but who knows where your book will take you, it may well be something to consider in the future. A paid influencer doesn't have to be a celebrity, they can be someone who is influential in only your area of expertise and as such may not cost as much as you think.

AFFILIATES

Affiliates are something I have been noticing more and more of lately, especially around software. Generally, you pay someone a fee or commission to promote your product or service. This can be a very powerful way to reach a large audience but it will depend on your product or service as to whether or not it is useful.

EMAIL DIRECT MARKETING

Email Direct Marketing (EDM) is the term used for when you pay someone else who has your potential customers/readers on their email list. They will not be a direct competitor but someone who shares your tribe. For example: we could send an EDM to a writing centre's list promoting our services. And it would be clearly indicated that it was a paid service. EDMs are a great way to effectively reach your niche.

Think about what industry bodies have your target market. Do you know someone who offers a service in the same field that has a large email list? If you already have a substantial list, is there someone you could run a cross promotion with?

BOOKBUB

BookBub is a service that is free to readers, helping millions discover great deals on acclaimed ebooks. It also provides publishers and authors a way to drive sales and find new fans.

How It Works

Members sign up for free and receive daily emails alerting them to the best free and heavily discounted ebooks that match their selected interests, as selected by BookBub's editorial team.

Process to Apply/Promotion Requirements

As an author you need to meet the following requirements to be even considered for promotion, and it only applies to ebooks.

- Free or discounted by 50 per cent of the RRP.
- The best deal available for the past 90 days or the near future.
- Error free, this includes typos, grammar and formatting.
- A limited time offer.
- A full-length book and work of nonfiction must be at least 100 pages.
- Widely available.
- Will only feature once every six months.

Meeting all these criteria does not guarantee you will be considered. The selection process is highly competitive as they receive anywhere from 100 to 300 submissions per day and will only consider taking on 10–15 per cent of the titles. They do this to ensure quality and to not overwhelm their members.

If this is something you feel would benefit your marketing and promotion, these are the areas BookBub suggests you focus on:

- Make the deal price as competitive as possible.
- Accumulate 'Reader Reviews'.
- Professionally designed cover optimised for your genre.
- Critical reviews from influential reviewers or well-known authors.
- Award Winners.
- Optimise your product page description.
- Upload and discount your book on all online book retailers, not just Amazon.

- Include all regions in your submission.
- Be flexible with your promotion date.

If BookBub do not select you on the first submission you can reapply at a later date. If you are selected to be a BookBub featured deal, while exciting it can be expensive. Costs range from AUD $100 up to $3500 for an international 'Featured' deal. This varies depending on the genre and the price for the ebook. At the time of print, a book in the General Nonfiction ranged from $363 for a free book to $1815 for a $2+ ebook.

Author Profile

Another bonus to being selected as a Featured Deal is you can claim your free author profile. This allows all authors to showcase their work on BookBub's website, including other books that have been written by the author but have not been a Featured Deal.

Whether or not you choose to look at doing this kind of paid promotion will greatly depend on who your target audience is, what the end outcome of publishing your book is, and if high book sales are a primary concern to you.

There is little point in paying for international promotion if the primary purpose of your book is to get clients through the doors and can only be done on a local basis. If, however, the purpose of the book is to bring attention to an issue, for example: the environment and you have organic products that you sell online, this could be a very worthwhile promotion.

What has been covered in this chapter is only a small selection of paid advertising options. This is an ever-expanding market and will change and update on an on-going basis. Be creative and start to take notice of what catches your attention.

TOP
tips

1. Define where your niche is, where your target market is spending their time and run ad campaigns there.

2. Set up an autoresponder for targeted email campaigns.

3. Run split tests to see what works.

4. Study the analytics to see what works.

5. Think outside the box – who can you cross promote with?

6. Who can you pay to send an email to their list?

7. Who already has your target market?

8. Be creative and spend your dollars wisely.

{

CHAPTER 20

Earnt: referrals, interviews, media

It can be argued that the best form of promotion is by referral. Ask yourself how often do you talk to friends and colleagues about a new service or product you are considering buying? How often do you choose one that has been referred? I am guessing more often than not.

In this chapter you will learn not only how to ask for referrals and testimonials, but also how to gain maximum benefit from them, and how to approach the media and become a 'go to' source for interviews, as well as learning about the power of speaking engagements.

WHAT IS A REFERRAL?

A referral is one of the most powerful tools to help build your profile. They are a third-party endorsement that establishes your credibility. One of the best, most consistent ways to get referrals or testimonials is to deliver an outstanding product or service, going above and beyond what your customer expects of you. The other is to ask for them.

A referral can take the form of a customer story, or it could be about how you deliver results. For example: if your clients are home builders or renovators, the story could include a 'before and after shot' of their house, or a picture of someone moving into their new home. These customer stories are a great way to develop your profile and there are two main types:

Stories told and shared by your customer and include:

- Reviews on online review sites such as Yelp.com, online store reviews, restaurant reviews, book reviews and so on.
- Reviews on personal blogs, Twitter, Facebook and other social media platforms.
- Word of mouth.

It is important to remember that these customer stories aren't always positive. Sometimes you can't avoid negative reviews; however, it is how you handle the situation that can make all the difference in securing a good outcome for all.

Stories generated and shared by you can include:

- Customer testimonials – these can be featured on your website and in brochures and other marketing materials. These are typically brief comments provided by your customer. Video testimonials are a popular way of sharing people's experiences.
- Case studies – these are often longer stories that go into more detail about your customer's journey with you. These can be featured on your website and in promotional brochures and other marketing documents.

In order to capture these powerful customer stories, you need a system because if you don't ask for one at the right time it is highly unlikely you will get one.

COLLECTING STORIES

How can you collect data that is powerful, compelling and useable? By asking the right questions. If you ask – what was their experience like – the customer is more than likely going to answer with a quick 'great thanks'. This answer is not powerful and definitely not compelling.

Ask these four questions to get the best results:

1. What has been the best part of your experience?
2. What areas can we improve on?
3. Would you recommend us to your friends? If yes, what would you say?
4. Can we use your comments on our website and in our marketing materials?

By asking these four simple questions, you are more likely to gain some powerful testimonials? You can have this set up using a free survey tool such as Survey Monkey or Survey Gizmo. This is both easy for your customer and easy for you to compile the data.

INCREASING THE RESPONSE RATE

How you ask for feedback will determine the response rate. Just stating you are grateful for their feedback and providing a link might be okay and get some results, but a more compelling call to action is:

> *Thank you for choosing to do business with us. We're constantly looking at ways to improve our services and would love your feedback on your recent experience. We want to ensure we're providing services that suit your needs, so if you have time to complete our 1-minute survey, we'd really appreciate it. You can do it here.*

REVIEWING THE DATA AND EXTRACTING THE GOLD

There is no point in wasting both your time and your customer's time if you aren't going to review the data and use it. There is gold in this data, but only if used.

How you can use these stories:

- Highlight a customer success story on Facebook.
- Feature a customer testimonial in a newsletter.
- Feature a case study on a blog post.
- Feature customer stories and case studies on your website.

Referrals are a powerful way to build credibility and trust with your customers. It brings a human touch to your online presence.

RAISING YOUR PROFILE IN MAINSTREAM MEDIA

Pitching to mainstream media is a great way to build your profile but requires a plan of action. For the greatest success don't pitch to the media until you are prepared:

- Be findable.
- Have callouts and media alerts activated.
- Ensure your photography and visuals are sorted.
- Understand media timing.
- Define your media plan.

BE FINDABLE

By this I mean, is there an easy media section on your website? Look at websites that do this well – HerBusiness and Valerie Khoo are great examples of what to include. Make it clear what topics you can comment on. If you have phone and email details listed, check them regularly. If the media makes contact with you for a comment on something that is currently happening, they want a quick response and getting back to them several days after will be too late.

CALLOUTS AND MEDIA ALERTS

Sign up for callouts and media alerts. One example is – sourcebottle. com.au. This site is free to sign up and they will email you twice a day with different callouts that fit your profile. If you are responding to a callout, provide as much detail as possible that is tailored for the callout. Don't send a generic response.

PHOTOGRAPHY AND VISUALS

Now is a good time to review your professional photos. If you are responding to mainstream media it is likely they will call for photos to be included, and if you only have a headshot this is all they can use. Think about getting a few different photos in both landscape and portrait that are full body shots, not just the boring studio photos.

UNDERSTANDING MEDIA TIMING

If you are planning to pitch your book to mainstream media it is vital you understand the lead times that are involved. This is especially important for print magazines.

Newspapers

What	Being Put to Bed	Developing Stories
Newspapers print and online (general news section)	The day before	3–4 days
Online non-news sections of sites – e.g. Daily Life, Essential Kids, Essential Baby	The day before	Some stories are developed as late as the day before in order to be topical. Other stories can be planned 2–3 weeks in advance

Newspaper sections – e.g. My Career, Media, Drive, TV Guide	2 weeks before	4–8 weeks before
Newspaper colour magazine supplements	4 weeks before	9–12 weeks before

Magazines

What	Being Put to Bed	Developing Stories
Glossy monthly women's magazine	3 months before	5 months before
Other monthly magazines	3 months before	4 months before
Monthly trade or industry magazines	1 month before	2–3 months before
Weekly magazines – e.g. WHO, Woman's Day	1 month before	9–12 weeks before
Weekly business magazines	2–3 weeks before	2 months

Bearing in mind these lead times, it is important to plan story ideas well in advance to pitch to the media. You are not going to have success at getting your book launch in the media if you only start pitching the idea a week prior to your launch.

YOUR MEDIA PLAN

Before you start sending out media releases to everyone and anyone, you want to make sure you are targeting the right media. The idea of getting media coverage is not to boost your ego, although this might be a by-product, but to reach more customers and build both your business and your profile.

So the first thing to do is go back and review your target market:

- Who are they?
- How old are they?

- Where do they live?
- What are their interests?
- What media do they read and listen to?

This last point is where you should focus your attention. Really narrow down where your customers are, don't just look at men's magazines, narrow it down and get specific.

PITCH YOUR STORY TO JOURNALISTS AND EDITORS

A pitch is when you contact a journalist or editor to try and get them interested in your story. Do your research and find out who the right person is to email. Call the publication and ask for an email, don't just send it to a generic email.

Publications receive hundreds, if not thousands, of media releases and you need to follow these three steps to even get yours looked at:

- Send your release to a real person.
- Include a tailored media release.
- Include a short personalised note.

There is no guarantee that anyone will run with your story, but if you make everything as easy as possible for the journalist they are more likely to consider you.

BOOK REVIEWS

One thing you should do when the box of printed books arrives, is to send out review copies for readers who write book reviews on either their own book review websites, Goodreads and Amazon, and any other industry-related publications that your target audience would read. Most publications should include a book review section for books relevant to your industry. Be prepared in advance by preparing a list of publications and contacts that are interested in reviewing your specific genre. Before publishing this book, I created a list of reviewers that included:

- Andrew Griffiths, Author and Speaker
- Alison Vidotto; Push Leadership
- Katie Woods; CEO Qld Writers Centre

Forward potential reviewers a copy of your book and be sure to include a note thanking them and asking for a review.

CONTACTING A PUBLICIST

If gaining media attention is paramount to your book's success, then it might be worthwhile contacting a publicist. The cost varies depending on who you hire but it may be money well spent.

Overview on what should be prepared:

- A Media Release – tailor this for each outlet and make it topical, giving journalists a story angle. It should be no longer than one page, as they are very busy people. Write it like an article and include key information about your book such as price, release date and ISBN.
- Media List – prepare a list of relevant media and contact details of the relevant editor or assistant editor.

While all the topics discussed in this chapter are free, they do take a considerable amount of time. Planning to get them right and done properly can be a very powerful way to increase your profile. You will also find that once you start the easier it will be. When you have established a profile and the media knows you are a reliable source, they will contact you. It is a small world nowadays and news travels fast.

TOP *tips*

1. Collect testimonials.

2. Set up a quick survey for customer feedback.

3. Promote testimonials on social media and website.

4. Create a media profile.

5. Create a media page on your website.

6. Subscribe to SourceBottle and other media callout sites.

7. Write a media release.

8. Research media outlets and the relevant journalists.

9. Send copies of your book to book reviewers.

SECTION FOUR

{ Leverage your book for
long-term success }

{
CHAPTER 21
Now for the fun part – your first book launch

There is no right or wrong to how you choose to launch your book. It will depend on what you want to get out of your book launch. Your desired outcome could be purely based on celebrating your fantastic achievement of becoming a published author with friends and family. For others it is a chance to build buzz and excitement about your business and your book.

In this chapter you will find key tips on what you should think about when planning your celebration. Whatever you decide, this is your time to shine and to pat yourself on the back for accomplishing your dream!

CELEBRATION STYLE
The release of your book is the perfect time to celebrate. In some cases, you may have spent years writing your book, for others there have been frantic months writing, editing, designing and publishing your book. The launch of your book is a time to celebrate with family and friends. You have achieved something many people only dream or talk about doing.

A successful launch all comes down to planning, planning,

planning. As with any event, careful, well thought out plans will help ensure you have a successful book launch, and also have fun. Remember success for one author is very different to what success looks like for others. A book launch is not the time to wing it.

The most important step in the planning process is to decide what type of celebration you want. One that is a big party with family and friends that's main purpose is fun? Or would you prefer one that includes friends and family, as well as clients, business colleagues and potential partners? The purpose in this scenario is also to have fun, but the main focus is on providing you and your business with another platform to promote your book. Either option is great, just don't combine the two.

VENUE

Book launch styles and venues vary as much as weddings do. I have been to book launches in bookstores, outside garden restaurants, and function rooms. Some events include a handful of people, others include hundreds.

If you have a book on a topic that lends itself to a particular location/venue, look at holding your book launch there. For example: if you have written a book on sailing hold your launch at the yacht club. Or hold your cookbook launch at a restaurant where demonstrations can be held.

You are only limited by your imagination and your budget. Depending on your time constraints and skills, you may decide to outsource all the planning or do it all yourself.

FORMAT

Once again, there are no set rules but remember people have come to your launch to help you celebrate your achievement and they will expect you to say a few words, even if you hate speaking in public.

Generally, a friend or colleague will say a few kind words about you and your book. It helps if they have already read your book. Then they will introduce you, and this is a great opportunity to talk about your book, perhaps reading something from your introduction. Don't forget to let everyone know where they can buy your book and thank them for helping you celebrate.

BOOK SALES

In the planning phase of publishing your book, something you should organise is printing books in advance for the launch. Ensure you have plenty of copies available for sale on the night. You can organise a bookshop to come and do this for you, but remember you will be paying them between 45 to 50 per cent of the selling price to do this.

Generally, there will be one of your friends or family that will be more than happy to help out on the night.

It is a nice personal touch to conduct a book signing on the night where you are available to sign books, including a personal message or sign copies in advance.

PUBLICITY

It is a good idea to try and gain some media exposure around your book launch. Media exposure helps build momentum and buzz around both the launch and your book. It also builds credibility around your book, sometimes having the added bonus of validating what you have achieved to friends and family. In some cases, family can be your worst critic.

Don't just send out a generic email to all and sundry, this is a sure fire way to get your email deleted. Do some research into what publications would be interested in your story. Are you a good fit for their readers? Make the journalist's job easier by clearly identifying why their readers would be interested in your book and its launch. If you are a service business, approach your local newspaper. Think of online and print publications that write about your topic.

This is not something that can be left to the last minute. Approaching the media takes time, and for the best results approach them well in advance. See Chapter 20 for a detailed list of timeframes.

PERMANENT RECORD

Having a record of your book launch isn't just a nice thing to have for the memories, they can also be used in your marketing. Professional photos of you and your business colleagues are a great tool to use on social media and your website.

Do you know any celebrities that you could invite to come along to the launch? If you don't you could always write to one who you think would be interested in your topic. Don't forget to include a copy of your book, if available. What is the worst they can say – 'no thanks'?

The other thing I have seen done is a video of the presentation being used as part of a video series on the author's web page and social media. If you don't have photos or a video, you have nothing to use. Having these available in the future allows for options.

THANK YOU GIFTS

You may think a free book is a good 'thank you gift', but you will find your friends and family are happy to buy your books as a way of 'thanking' you.

So a good thing to include as a gift is a bookmark. Have these printed when you have the book printed. Have your designer design this when doing the cover, that way there will be a common theme.

Other ideas include:

- Pens
- Glasses cleaner

- Drink bottles
- USB drives
- Bags

If you are planning on including a 'thank you gift', try and think of something that won't be thrown away and will be seen by people beyond the launch.

At the end of the day there are a thousand and one ways you can hold your book launch and ultimately there are no hard and fast rules. It can take the style and format that suits you and your industry best. No matter what you choose to do, do something that celebrates your amazing achievement. Many people talk about writing a book but few accomplish this dream. Be proud, you have created something that most only dream about. Well Done.

TOP
tips

Event Planner Checklist

1. Number of guests.

2. Venue.

3. MC.

4. Party or function.

5. Catering food and alcohol.

6. Time and date of launch.

7. Pre-order books for sales.

8. Write personalised media releases.

9. Send media releases.

10. Build momentum on social media.

11. Book photographer.

12. Book video production.

13. Organise a 'thank you gift'.

14. Plan speech.

15. Organise outfit.

16. Have fun.

{

CHAPTER 22

Using your book to grow your income and diversify your business

The purpose of writing a business book is often very different to that of other genres. Your main purpose in publishing your book isn't about selling hundreds of thousands of copies; however, while this would be wonderful, it is certainly not the norm.

Firstly, what defines a bestselling book? In Australia, there is no magic number of book sales to be reached before you can declare yourself a bestselling author, but in traditional publishing that figure is generally between three to four thousand books. What classifies as a 'bestselling book' on Amazon will depend on your category and the number of books you sell on a given day.

Your book is a marketing tool for you and your business. As mentioned before, it is a business card on steroids, and as such, book sales are not generally the primary motivator. In fact, you will probably end up buying a considerable percentage of the books yourself to give to potential clients and partners.

However, if having high numbers of book sales is important, there are a number of ways that you can promote your book. One thing to take into consideration when doing any paid promotion is to do your research. There are plenty of online sites and books claiming to have a fool-proof way of promoting and selling your book. If it sounds too good to be true, then it probably is. As with most things in business, research is the key to success.

This chapter covers the various ways you can promote your book and ensure you reach your target audience.

PUBLICITY

When factoring in marketing and publicity for your book, you could consider running an advertisement in a publication, probably costing in excess of $10,000 for a half-page ad. Or you could spend the time writing to individual publications explaining why their readers would like to read about your business and your book and get a full-page article written and published at no cost to you, other than your time, ultimately saving you $10,000.

As mentioned in previous chapters, don't send out a generic email to all media, do your research into which publications would benefit from your story. Editors and publishers have hundreds, if not thousands of emails dropping into their inboxes daily. Make sure your subject line is eye-catching and thought-provoking, to ensure you have a better chance of them even opening your email and reading it. Do not use the subject line, 'Book Launch' or 'Media Opportunity'. Make sure you have a hook – answer a problem their readers have. Test out a couple of different subject lines and see which ones get the best response.

Remember, don't take a lack of response personally. Rewrite what you are emailing and who you are targeting, and keep on trying. It might be that your subject line isn't hooking the editor or you are targeting the wrong publications.

Any published article can then be repurposed on your social media and websites. Being mentioned in the media will increase the opportunity of being published in other media outlets. Clients love to know they are working with businesses that appear in the media. It gives you credibility and increases your influence in your industry. Ensure you mention any media press on your website and social media.

REACHING OUT PAST OUR NETWORK

We all have someone in our sights that we would love to work with – our ideal client or partner. Or it could be someone you greatly admire who you would love to have acknowledge you and your business. Having a book published is the ideal way to reach out to them. Just send them a copy.

However, don't sent them any ordinary copy, sign your book and include a personal message and present it in a spectacular manner. And whatever you do, do not send it in an ordinary envelope that has the potential to arrive damaged. The time and the small expense to package your book in a way that says you care about your book, you value it and the message you have written, makes a powerful statement. It is like you are sending a gift. Also include your bookmark and any other promotional material you have printed.

Depending on the topic of your book, you could include any of the following:

- Bookmark
- Tea bag/box
- Inspirational quote
- Calendar
- Box of chocolate
- Scented candle
- Extra copy of your book to give away
- Bath salts
- Sample products

Once again, you are limited by your own imagination. Just think – if someone sent you a book, are you more likely to remember fondly receiving an unsigned book that turns up in a drab envelope, or will you remember the book that is signed and is beautifully packaged as a gift?

Think about the experience you are creating and how you want to be remembered. You are sending what you want people to think of you and your business, and you will get far more value from being considered *great* rather than just good.

INFORMATION TOOL DEFINING THE TYRE KICKERS

Writing and publishing a book is a great tool for lead generation. When potential clients contact you, offer to send them a complimentary copy of your book. This is an expense, but it can be factored into your marketing budget.

You have no doubt written about what to look for when choosing your service or product, and the reader will be able to determine if they like your style of doing business. They will gain an insight into you as a person, what your values are, and in essence if you are aligned in what outcome you are working to achieve.

Anyone who doesn't work with you and chooses your competitors was most likely not a good fit for you and your business. And you never know, they may well give your book to someone else who does become a client.

Remember, your book will not resonate with everyone and there will always be tyre kickers no matter what business you are in.

SAMPLE CHAPTERS

A great way to allow readers to see if they will find value in your book is by offering free sample chapters as a download from your website. More often than not people will come back and buy your book. I know I have done this with books before, as the free download enabled me to get an insight into the author's writing style and whether the content has value. In this time-poor era, you are not only asking readers to pay money for your book, but to also pay with their time by reading it.

SPEAKING ENGAGEMENTS

A great way to build your profile and share your expertise is by speaking at events and conferences. Having a book published is a great way to secure speaking engagements. The perceived credibility you gain by being introduced as a published author should not be underestimated.

I am not suggesting you start out by talking in front of thousands of people if the idea terrifies you – you can start small. Communicating effectively can be difficult if you are nervous or ill prepared. Think about local groups or meetups in your area, and offer to speak at these for free which will give you valuable experience in honing your speaking technique.

If you are serious about adding speaking engagements as a regular part of your working calendar, it may be helpful to work with a speaking coach. Another way to prepare is to practise at home and have someone record you and watch this back. It is amazing what you pick up when you watch yourself – you'll notice things that you had no idea you were doing subconsciously.

The benefits of speaking engagements are varied and not limited to the event itself and include:

- Being featured on the event website, sometimes for months before the event.
- Being promoted to the event's database of prospects. Even if they don't attend the event you are potentially being promoted

to thousands of people who you would not otherwise have access to.

- Have your message broadcast through live tweeting from the event, as well as reviews/summaries of your session in post-event blog posts.
- Additional exposure if you upload your presentation to Slideshare.
- If the event is recorded, this is additional exposure on the organiser's website, social media and so on.

Writing a business book and leveraging it well will change your life. For most entrepreneurs who have written a book the number of book sales is not the primary goal. The book's purpose is to help build your profile and industry credibility. So when looking at how to leverage your book think about how it will affect your bottom line, not just the numbers of books sold. And remember, now is the time to be proud and tell everyone about your book.

TOP
tips

1. Research media outlets and make a list of which ones have your target market.

2. Write personalised emails to try and gain publicity.

3. Think about who you would like to know and send them a book.

4. Presentation of your book is important.

5. Think about what else you could include to make a fantastic first impression.

6. Contact local groups and offer to speak at a function.

CHAPTER 23

Author network

What is an author network and do you need one? In reality, this section should really be the first chapter of the book, but hopefully you are reading this book at the commencement of your writing journey and this chapter will stay fresh in your mind.

This chapter will help you clarify not only what an author network is, but who is in yours. By the end of the chapter you will be surprised by how extensive your network probably is.

WHAT IS AN AUTHOR NETWORK?

An author network is people you know either directly or indirectly, and groups that you can reach out to help promote your book. The simplest way to define your author network is to mind map all the people, business groups either physical or via social media that you belong to, alliances you have, business partnerships and industry bodies you belong to.

Place yourself in the centre of your mind map and link out to everyone you know. If you know someone who is connected to an influencer in your field, include them. Have a discussion on how you can make this connection. Bear in mind, you will have published a book and this is a wonderful way to make a meaningful introduction.

Don't be afraid to include the most tentative connections as the power of a published book has far-reaching influence. Creating your mind map is a powerful tool in cementing in your mind who is in your network.

Building your author network is not about being a 'show pony' screaming 'look at me, look at me'. It is about sharing your industry knowledge and experience with people who will either directly or indirectly find value in what you have written.

As Australians, high achievers often suffer from 'tall poppy syndrome' and this feeling of being judged for our perceived success does not help in our ability to reach out. But to be a successful entrepreneur, you not only need to learn how to do this, but you need to embrace the process.

Start thinking of articles you can write to submit to the media or business groups you belong to. Think about which groups you belong to on social media, for example: Facebook and LinkedIn. Start by researching what other people are writing and what articles seem to get the greatest response, and start submitting your own articles. Two online platforms that are worth looking into are Smallville and HerBusiness. Both platforms attract a wide-ranging audience that you can reach out to. When submitting articles ensure that you have included a call to action.

Thinking back to the previous chapter and partnerships you can forge, are there any prospects here that can circulate your books as free promotion? This can be either print or digital depending on your market and your budget. Doing a digital free promotion has no outlay other than the initial cost of production, but it lacks the impact that a print book has.

If doing a digital promotion, include the call to action to buy a discounted print book from your website. This allows you to capture data of readers who resonated with your book.

THERE WILL STILL BE 'HATERS'

One of the most important and challenging parts of creating and developing your author network is dealing with the fact that not everyone will like what you have written or agree with you. Remember though, that if everyone did it would probably be a very short, very bland and boring book.

You have written this book to connect and share with your niche – your tribe – and this is not all encompassing. There will be the haters out there but most importantly there will be people who gain significant insights by reading your book and your message.

Chances are few people will have written a business book in your field and this will help you stand out from your competitors and peers. Don't be afraid to share your book with your competitors, you have not written this book for them and it is not full of industry jargon but will more than likely be something their clients resonate with.

Clarissa Rayward heads up the Brisbane Family Law Centre and is author of *Splitsville*, often has her competitors buying her books to give to their clients. There is nothing else on the market that is similar to Clarissa's book and it has value whether or not you are a client of Clarissa's.

But doesn't that just help my competitors? Well, yes, in a way, but it could also be seen as helping your industry. Especially if you belong to an industry that people generally regard with a degree of mistrust, for example: lawyers and real estate agents. Keep in mind who your competitor's client will remember as being the 'author' and 'influencer'. Whose book are they going to have on their bookshelf?

Whose book are they going to give to a friend?

The wonderful thing about writing and publishing, especially a printed book, is that a book is something of value to share, it shows the world you value what you do to the extent that you spent valuable time and money writing and publishing your book. You value your message and the significance it will hold for your readers.

This is something to bear in mind when developing your author network. Don't just include people you know well, think further, think about the value your book is going to have and who will find value in it.

TOP
tips

1. Mind map everyone you know and their connections.

2. If you would like to connect with someone, ask yourself who do you know that can help?

3. Write and submit articles to publications that your customers read.

4. Build your network by being visible both on and offline.

{ *Conclusion*

I hope that you have been able to learn some of the strategies and tools on how to write, publish and leverage your business book.

Remember that now is not the time to listen to the voices in your head saying, 'What will people say?', 'Who am I to write a book?', 'Nobody will read it anyway'. We all have these voices talking in us, and sometimes they whisper and other times they shout, but we do have a choice as to whether or not we listen to them. This is something I understand first hand as I have spent years having conversations with my own head, where a great many arguments have taken place. And sometimes I win, and sometimes the 'little voice' does.

This is what Alison Vidotto had to say about publishing her book *22 Leadership Fundamentals*:

> *Writing the book was a great way to really focus on and articulate exactly what my fundamental beliefs are about leadership. From there we have gone on to develop our manifesto, mission statement etc. It has also been a great marketing tool, to introduce who we are and what we do. We provide every member of*

*our training with a copy of the book as a point of reference long
after the training is over.*

If you have ever asked yourself: 'What can I do to make my business more profitable, share my experience and stand out from the
crowd?' then writing a business book is one way to do this. If you
have reached the end of the book then I know you must be serious
about sharing your knowledge, experience and story with the world.

Don't feel overwhelmed, go back to the beginning of the book and
follow the stages in the writing and publishing process, and before
you know it you will have a manuscript ready to send to the editor.

I wish you all the best of luck with your writing journey and I look
forward to meeting you along the road.

{ Bonuses

For more great bonuses, templates, checklists and guides visit:
www.independentink.com.au

{ Feedback

I would love to hear from you and if you enjoyed reading this
book please consider leaving a review. You can find me on our
Facebook page www.facebook.com/independentink.publishing
or on LinkedIn au.linkedin.com/in/annwilson4

{ Independent Ink

If you would like more help and information on self-publishing
from Ann Wilson, visit www.independentink.com.au, email
ann@independentink.com.au or call us on 07 3398 9365.

{ *Glossary*

ADVANCE COPIES

The first few copies of your book sent from the printer to the publisher for approval, before the bulk of the books are printed. These should be checked carefully.

BIBLIOGRAPHY/REFERENCE

A bibliography is a list of all materials/resources used in the research of your book. These are listed alphabetically at the end of the book in a separate bibliography section. Generally, these are listed as the author name (surname followed by initial); year of publication; title of works (in italics); publisher; place of publication.

An example:

Wilson, A, 2015, *Independent Ink Terminology*, Post Pre-press, Carina.

References are resources from written works referred to directly in your book. References are usually listed alphabetically at the end of the book in a separate reference section. The listing is the same as for a bibliography.

BINDING

The action of folding a printed sheet then sewing, stapling or gluing these into a book. Printers use different names but paperbacks are usually 'perfect bound' or 'perfect bind'.

BLEED

This is the off page area printed to allow for minor inaccuracies in trimming. Generally anything intended to print right up to the edge of the page is extended and bleeds about 5mm beyond the intended edge of the trimmed page.

COLOUR RESOLUTION

Colour resolution is the amount of information in dots that make up an image. In publishing, colour resolution refers to any colour images in the book. These can be photos, colour drawings, graphs, tables etc. To achieve a high-quality image when your book is printed, images should be supplied at 300ppi (pixels per inch) at the minimum. 600ppi is required for line drawings. This can also be referred to as dpi (dots per inch).

DINKUS

A dinkus is a symbol used to indicate a minor break in the text. It can be an asterisk, 3 consecutive asterisks or any relevant small symbol.

DROP CAPS

A drop cap is the first letter of a chapter that is created in either a larger font size or using a different font. The use of a drop cap is a personal choice and is only used for visual appeal.

ELLIPSIS

Meaning 'omission'. In grammar, an ellipsis is the omission of a word needed to complete the construction or sense. In writing, an ellipsis is the name used for three dots . . .

EM DASH (EM RULE)

A long dash (—) used in punctuation. The choice between en and em dashes, and the decision to space them, is up to the typographer or author. Recently spaced en dashes have become more popular.

EN DASH (EN RULE)

A dash (–) that indicates a closed range of values such as dates, times, numbers or acts as a hyphen connecting adjectives or prefixes to open compounds. Also used as a dash between phrases.

FOLIOS

Publishers and printers refer to page numbers as the folios. The folios can be centred or outside margin at the top or bottom of the page. There is no correct placement of folios – it is a personal preference.

FONT

A font means 'a complete set of type carrying a given size of a given typeface', which comprises upper and lower case characters, numerals, punctuation marks and a range of special characters. The terms: bold; italics; bold italics etc. are referred to as 'font styles'. When talking about font you will be asked about type size. For example: 10/12pt (ten on twelve point) refers to the type size and the distance from the baseline of one line to the baseline of the next.

A printer's measure for a point is equal to approximately 0.3mm. The 10pt refers to the body height of the type, measuring from the highest ascender to the foot of the lowest descender, plus a small overhang of the body to allow for a space between each line of characters. The 12pt indicates an extra 2pt space between the lines. This 2pt space is also referred to as the 'leading'. This is a term dating back to when books were handset in metal type. If the typesetter thought the text looked better with extra space between the lines, strips of lead were then inserted, hence the name 'leading'.

FONT SELECTION

Brilliant typography should be something that is not noticed, therefore we always recommend using a simple, easy-to-read font. It is best to choose a font that is available in various weights and styles including bold, italics and bold italics.

GUTTERS

A gutter is the inside margin or blank space between two facing pages. This extra space allows for the binding of the book. The amount of space or gutter size varies depending on the book binding method chosen.

HYPHENATION

The choice to use hyphenation is a personal one. The use of hyphenation ensures that lines do not appear gappy or tight. This is referred to as a discretionary hyphen or soft hyphen. All hyphenation should be checked to ensure that no bad word breaks appear or that there is no hyphenation at the end of a page. It is visually unappealing to have too many hyphens on a page, we aim for no more than 5 per page.

ILLUSTRATIONS/CAPTIONS

A caption is the relevant information about a photo or illustration. The placement of the caption can be either below or to the side of the image. This will depend on the page layout.

IMPRINT PAGE

The imprint page or copyright page is usually backing the title page on the verso (often the fourth page) on which the copyright notice, publisher, ISBN and other details about the publication are printed.

LAYOUT

Traditional books have always been produced with justified text. This means that all words in all lines are spaced out so that the first word aligns with the left margin and the last word with the right margin.

The first line of each paragraph is also indented. The pattern of opening indents and short lines at the end of paragraphs helps enable the reader to visualise the logical shape of the text by emphasising paragraph breaks.

Alternative page layouts are flush left/ragged right and flush right/ ragged left.

These can be useful for specific purposes, such as poetry and prose, and to distinguish letters or emails within the text. Flush left can avoid large spaces between words and excessive hyphenation. However, it can tend to look amateurish and old-fashioned if used over a large extent of text. It can also be difficult to read and keep track of paragraphs.

LINE LENGTH

The length of line (i.e. the number of characters per line) and type size is important due to how we recognise words and read. The longer the line, the more effort is required to stay on track. Independent Ink recommends having a line length of between 50 and 70 characters.

MANUSCRIPT (MS)

Text delivered by an author. Usually a word file supplied either on disc or electronically, but may be typewritten or even handwritten.

MARGINS

The margin refers to the space at the top, bottom and either side of the text on the page. It is the empty space between the trim (where the paper is cut) and the text on the page. Sometimes the headers and footers are in the margins.

ORPHANS/WIDOWS

A widow is the last line of a paragraph that appears at the top of a page, and an orphan is the first line of a paragraph that appears at the bottom of a page. Sometimes it is vice versa, depending who you talk to. It is visually more appealing to avoid having orphans and widows if possible. Sometimes this is unavoidable unless the text is edited. An orphan is also when the last word of a paragraph is on a line by itself, especially at the base of a page.

PAGE PROOFS

First Pages

On completion of the typesetting a set of first page proofs are supplied either as a printed copy, PDF or both. These are used to proofread and mark up any correction/changes that are to be taken in.

Corrections

Corrections, additions or deletions are taken into the typeset file from the page proofs. These can either be handwritten or marked up in the PDF. If the manuscript has been edited prior to typesetting these should be minimal.

Final Pages

These are the final page proofs to be approved before a final PDF is supplied to the printer.

PAGINATION

Another item to think about is the pagination and page extent. In the case of a printed book, this will be influenced by the number of pages required by the printer. Printers work in sections and this will be in multiplies of 4, 12 or 16 pages. If you are printing the book yourself, you will need to confirm this with your printer. When counting your page extent, be mindful that you may also need to include:

Title Page
Imprint Page
Dedication
Contents
Acknowledgements
About the Author

A blank page can be inserted where necessary to reach the required number of pages.

PAPER SIZES see TRIM SIZE

PRINTING

Choice of paper, also referred to as 'stock', can be a technical issue and takes into account many preferences including, style, weight, bulk, colour and opacity. The following guidelines are here to help when talking to printers.

Papers

Art Papers: These are made with clay as a filler, which gives the paper a smooth finish that makes them particularly good for printing photographs.

Gloss Art: The production process produces a porcelain finish that gives spectacular results with colour printing; however, the amount of reflected light can make reading difficult. Gloss Arts paper is essentially wonderful for coffee table books.

Matt Art: Is a good compromise between the above two papers.

One-sided Art: Has a gloss finish on one side only, and is good for book jackets.

Coated: These are newsprints that are spray-coated with a clear enamel giving a gloss finish. Mainly used for cheap magazines, but they are sometimes used for books where there is a need for bright colour at a low cost.

Book printings: This is the term used for a large variety of papers that normal books are printed on. See below for more details.

Newsprints: Used for newspapers and cheap paperback books.

Paper (stock) is specified by type and weight. For example: 100 gsm Bookprint Matt – gsm stands for 'grams per square metre'.

Bookprint Choice

Colour: The main choices are ultra-whites, whites and creams. Compared to a white, ultra-white can have a bluish hue. Ultra-whites are best used for colour work and can be hard on the eye when reading text.

Finish: The terms wood and weave are about smoothness. Wood is a random fluff, and a good paper can be referred to as woodfree. Weave is a deliberate texture and this is what gives a lot of papers their character.

Bulk: Means thickness. The bulk will depend on the weight and style. The weight that gives this bulk varies. Generally 65 gsm is used for newsprint, 80 gsm for books and 100 gsm for art/colour books.

RECTO AND VERSO

The terms 'recto' and 'verso' are shortened from Latin and refer to the text written on the front and back of a page.

In an open book the left-hand page (even number page) is called the verso and the right-hand page (odd number page) is a recto page.

The general style in book publishing is to place the first page, and sometimes each chapter and section, on a recto page.

RUNNING HEADS

A running head is a heading printed at the top of each page of a book. It is personal choice whether to include running heads and if so what they will be. A standard format is often the author name on the verso page and the book title on the recto. When chapters have a title this can be used as a running head on the recto page with the book title on the verso. Can also be placed at bottom of page (ie Running Feet) which is often the case in Cookbooks.

SPECIFICATION see PRINTING

SPINE

The bound edge of the book.

SUBSIDIARY RIGHTS (SOME NOT EXCLUSIVE)

This is the right to produce or publish a product in different formats based on the original material. These include:

- Abridgment
- Amusement park or theme park
- Anthology
- Audio use
- Book club
- Collection
- Condensation
- Digest
- Direct-to-consumer sales
- Dramatic stage play
- First and second serialisation
- Foreign translations
- Games
- Graphic adaptation
- Interactive and multimedia electronic and/or digital use.
- Internet and online use
- Large print
- Merchandising
- Motion Picture
- Quotation
- Radio broadcast rights
- Television
- Video games

TITLE PAGE

The title page is often the third page and is always on a recto. The author's name, the title of the book, the series title and subtitle (if any) and the publisher's imprint logo all appear.

TRIM SIZE

The book size is referred to as the 'trim size'. This is the size where the book is trimmed at the final stages of production. The trim size you choose will depend on the style of your book and there are no hard and fast rules.

In today's book market paperbacks are referred to as A, B and C Formats. As a guide:

A Format is 181 x 111 mm
B Format is 198 x 128 mm
C Format is 234 x 153 mm

The exact size will depend on the printer and the machine used to trim the finished book.

UNIT COST

The unit cost is the cost to print each individual book. Generally this does not include the cost of editing, design and typesetting, as these are fixed costs and the number of print books is an unknown quantity.